WHEN *Love* DIED

THE TRUE STORY OF THE BRUTAL MURDER OF A WAR OF 1812 HERO THAT INVOLVED GREED, LIES AND TREACHERY

SHERRIE L. PLUTA

Fulton Books
Meadville, PA

Published by Fulton Books 2023

ISBN 979-8-88731-292-7 (paperback)
ISBN 979-8-88731-293-4 (digital)

Printed in the United States of America

To my family, whose support was never ending, and to the Boston Historical Society for allowing me unfettered access to their collections.

Preface

Urban legends—every town has one or two. Urban legends exist all over the country. Strange disappearances, haunted bridges, murderous rampages in days gone by, stories of witches, and mysterious stains appearing on wood floors in the shape of a screaming woman. Are they really true or just a legend?

In my hometown of Boston, New York, everyone who grew up there had heard the legend of the Love murder. It was a story about a man by the name of John Love, boarding for the winter with the Thayer family in the Boston Valley, who was then brutally murdered by the three Thayer brothers. They had borrowed money from Love, and when they found they could not pay him back, rather than losing their land to pay the debt, they decided to just do away with him. The story continued with the discovery of Love's dead body, the arrest of the three brothers, their trial and conviction, and their subsequent hangings in Niagara Square in Buffalo.

I was always intrigued by the story and often wondered if it was really true. Who was this John Love? Why did he have money to lend people in the early 1800s when cash money was as scarce as hen's teeth? Did three brothers actually plan his murder and carry it out? I wanted to see proof. The first proof I found was Love's grave marker. It was in the cemetery in the middle of town where my father would take us every year on Memorial Day to place flowers at the graves of his parents and his aunt and uncle who adopted him at the age of six when his parents succumbed to tuberculosis just a few months apart. The marker was located at the very front of the cemetery next to the road. Inscribed in the marker is the whole story, "John Love, trader, murdered December 15, 1824, in the Town of Boston, by Isiaac (*sic*), Israel, and Nelson Thayer, brothers who were hung from a common scaffold June 17, 1825."

But my curiosity went beyond that. What did it mean "John Love, trader"? Where in the town of Boston did it happen? Who were these brothers that they could plan such a heinous crime? How was Love murdered? Where was the "common scaffold"? I needed answers, so I started a lifetime of research to find them.

When I went back to college in my fifties, I found a way to get some of my answers. Using the college's Inter-Library Loan system, I was able to find primary sources of the trial and found I could get free copies of the documents held by other institutions in New York State.

Next I joined the Boston Historical Society, so I could see if it held any clues. Inside the Historical Museum, there was a display on the Love murder on the first floor. There were photocopies of some broadsides, pamphlets which were handed out to spectators at the hangings in the display, and hung on the wall at the top of the display

was the original wooden grave marker, which reads "John Love, murdered by the Three Thayers, December 15, 1824."

I found out that this original marker started disappearing from the cemetery sometime in the 1940s and then reappearing sometime later, according to the testimony of the groundskeeper. After it disappeared and reappeared several times, the heavy granite marker referenced above was made and installed, and the original wooden marker was given to the Boston Historical Society for safekeeping. It is currently still on display in their museum.

As I researched the facts about John Love's murder, I tried to find more information on the man himself. Newspaper articles reporting on the murder held at the Boston History Museum from the time mentioned that he was an immigrant, possibly from Scotland, England, or Wales. I tried looking in Ancestry.com's database, but apparently, the name "John Love" was very common, much like Smith and Jones are today. Again, the newspaper articles said he was a man in his early thirties, and he was of small stature. But that was all I was able to glean from those sources. Then as if providential, I became aware of a new local book being released that would prove the "aha" moment I was looking for. The book, *Joseph Bennett of Evans and the Growing of New York's Niagara Frontier* by Kevin H. Siepel, was published by the Spruce Tree Press in Angola, New York, in 2006. I contacted the publisher and found a phone number for Mr. Siepel and arranged to meet with him. I had heard that John Love made an appearance in the life of Joseph Bennett.

Joseph Bennett was a multifaceted and multitalented individual who began life as the oldest son of Samuel and Sally Bennett in 1803 in interior Vermont. His path eventually took him to Western New York, where he made his mark as a farmer, construction contractor, businessman, public servant, sailor, and family man. He made his home in Evans, New York, and contributed to that town's footprint and development.

Siepel used Bennett's collections of his daily thoughts and daily life in the form of a diary he discovered to tell the story of this man's life. Bennett kept the diary all his life, and according to Siepel's Dedication at the front of the book, the diary was kept "to help young people learn about those that were here before them."

Of all the stories of his life, the one that garnered my attention the most was the fact that Bennett loved boats, and he loved sailing on the Great Lakes. Bennett's diary informs the reader that sometime in April of 1824, he bought a new boat, took a room at a local boarding house, and looked around for a sailor to help him man the new boat in the spring. He found a man by the name of John

Love, "a small wiry Scotsman…a man who claimed to have been at sea since running away from home at the age of ten." Love told young Bennett that he had served aboard the US frigate *Constitution,* also known as *Old Ironsides* in its famous actions against the *HMS Guerriere* and *HMS Java* during the War of 1812. Joseph took him aboard gladly and was pleased to find that he was indeed an excellent seaman.

This was the "smoking gun" of personal information on John Love's life I was looking for in my research. Newspaper articles of the hangings had mentioned that Love was indeed a seaman and that he wasn't born in America. And here was the proof from the man who hired him the same year he was murdered. This evidence also steered me to research Love's military background.

I found that there was a museum in the Charlestown, Massachusetts Navy Yard called the USS Constitution Museum dedicated to the ship and its history. The actual ship is in a dry dock next to the museum. I contacted them and started an email chain of conversations that opened my eyes even more about Love's past. They confirmed the fact that "Ordinary Seaman John Love reported aboard *Constitution,* having enlisted at Philadelphia." They even found that his battle station was as a powder passer on the berth deck, moving the charges from a magazine hatch where they were handed up to the next deck. Since the battles between the *Constitution* and the *HMS Guerriere* and *HMS Java* were so important to the cause of the war and proved to be deadly to many, survivors were awarded a stipend for their service in the amount of $42.12 and $42.30 for the two victories, representing about four month's pay for each. This showed that John Love was an actual war hero who was bludgeoned to death by three brothers who wouldn't pay him back for a loan!

So my eyes were opened to the actual existence and character of the "urban legend" of John Love that I grew up knowing. This led me next to proving the existence of the three Thayer brothers—Nelson, Isaac, and Israel Jr.

First I went to the 1820 Federal Census for the Town of Boston, New York, and found the "head of household" name of Israel Thayer in a group of other homeowners in North Boston. The census lists the following persons as being included in this household: "One free White male under ten years, one free White male between sixteen and eighteen, eight free White males of sixteen and under twenty-six including heads of families, one free White male of twenty-six and under forty-five including heads of families, one free White male of forty-five and upward including heads of families, one free White female under ten years, and one free White female of forty-five and upward including heads of families." If I assume that Israel (Sr.) and his wife were the two listed as being over forty-five years, that would leave seven free White males between sixteen and twenty-six years of age and two children under the age of ten. No names are listed in the 1820 census except the head of household, Israel Thayer (Sr.). So according to the Federal Census, the three brothers involved in the John Love slaying were only three of the seven free White males listed in the household. I was never able to find out who the other four were.

I then found a website that listed all the deaths due to convictions in a court of law for which death by hanging was the punishment that took place in Erie County in the nineteenth century. Now I usually trust government records, and I found the three brothers on the list, but the date of punishment was wrong. The website revealed: On July 17, 1825 (it should have read June 17, 1825), Isaac Thayer, Israel Thayer (Jr), and Nelson Thayer, who were all listed as farmers, were hanged (in Niagara Square) for the crime of "Murder-Robbery." Their ages are listed as nineteen for Isaac, twenty-one for Israel Thayer (Jr), and twenty-three for Nelson Thayer. I have confirmed the June 17, 1825 date with many other primary sources, and I am sure of its integrity.

The "*coup de gras*" that led me to the brothers' existence was found at the Boston Historical Museum, which consisted of the original arrest warrant signed by District Attorney H. B. Potter, dated April 19, 1825, for the arrest of Israel Thayer (Sr.), Israel Thayer (Jr.), and Isaac Thayer. The museum did not, however, have the original or a copy of the arrest warrant for Nelson Thayer, who was charged separately as it was determined that he was the one who actually swung the axe and delivered the death blow. It was thought at the time that

Israel Thayer Sr. must have also had a hand in the deed, but it was later proven that he was not guilty.

Erie County, ss.—The Court of *Oyer & Terminer* holden in and for the said county of Erie: To the Sheriff and Constables of the said county, and every of them, Greeting: In the name of the People of the State of New-York, we command you to arrest and TAKE *Israel Thayer Junior & Isaac Thayer Israel Thayer Junior*

who *stand* Indicted in the said Court for *having feloniously, wilfully & of their malice aforethought killed & murdered John Love*

and *them* forthwith to commit to the common gaol of the said county of Erie, and there safely to keep *them* until delivered by due course of law. Given under our hands and seals, in open-session, at the Court House in Buffalo, this   day of— in the year of our Lord one thousand eight hundred and twenty-

Witness William B. Rochester Esquire Circuit Judge for the Eighth Circuit the Nineteenth day of April in the year of our Lord one thousand eight hundred & twenty five—

J. A. Barker Clerk

A. S. Porter Dist Atty

With that bit of research being done, I found that the year of the hangings, 1825, was a very historic time in the Western New York area. I expanded my research again to include finding out what nineteenth-century history was all about in the area where I lived.

In the early 1800s, the Western New York area was sparsely settled by intrepid families who moved west to start new communities, find new farmland, and quench their thirst for adventure and wanderlust. The city of Buffalo, some twenty miles north of Boston, was just a village made up of a half dozen families. The village was located on the eastern edge of Lake Erie and had vast forests of hardwoods and pine trees and plenty of game for a family's sustenance. Flat meadows abounded to grow crops of corn and wheat and everything else needed for families to thrive. Only a few families braved the Boston Valley at first, slowly growing as the Holland Land Company, who owned most of the land in Western New York, surveyed the land and broke it into habitable parcels.

One such settler in the village of Buffalo was Judge Samuel Wilkeson. During the War of 1812, he was asked by the country's fledgling government to build a fleet of ships to be harbored there as a defensive stronghold against British ships coming down the Great Lakes. (Even though they strongly defended it, the British still got through and burned the village to the ground in 1813.) Wilkeson was an industrious sort as many of the early settlers had to be. In addition to his work for the government, he owned a general store and became the village's first Justice of the Peace. He would later be instrumental in making Buffalo the most important harbor in the Great Lakes.

In 1825, commerce between the East Coast and the interior was practically nonexistent. Travel was hazardous at best over dirt roads littered with tree stumps and wagon wheel trenches that threatened to cripple a wagon by falling into a trench and breaking a wheel. Settlers who needed to sell their crops were limited to roadside stands and whatever they could sell at a market in another village. Buying goods that were made in the east was expensive and took weeks to arrive. Tools for the farm were made by each settler in the ways his ancestors had been doing for generations.

Settlers complained to their government to do something about the horrid roads, and factories in the east complained that they needed to sell their wares in a more profitable way. The year 1825 was the year all that changed.

On October 26, 1825, the greatest engineering marvel of that century opened between Albany and Buffalo. The Erie Canal would prove a boon to manufacturing in the east and food production in the west.

It took fourteen years to build the canal from initial conception to completion. It was conceived as an essential and economically important project—debated by lawmakers and naysayers. It would cut the state of New York in half from east to west, and it traveled through 363 miles of forests, rocky cliffs, swamps, and open fields. It was a daunting task but a significant one. In 1810, then president Thomas Jefferson, who commissioned Meriwether Lewis and William Clark to explore and map the newly acquired Louisiana purchase, was heard to comment that he did not believe the Erie Canal could be constructed in his lifetime.

The length of the canal was divided into three sections to make construction more organized. The eastern section would start in the Hudson Valley by Albany. The workers, who consisted mostly of Irish immigrants, would work their way west crisscrossing along the Mohawk River until they reached Rome. Then the middle section of the canal, which was positioned between Rome, New York, and the Montezuma National Wildlife Refuge at the northern end of Cayuga Lake, would see dozens of new towns being built to house the hundreds of workers and see to their needs. The western terminus would be built last in no small part because there was disagreement over exactly which village would serve as the "end of the line." The disagreement was over whether the village of Buffalo should be the terminus, or the village of Black Rock, an independent town just a few miles to the north. Each settlement had advantages and disadvantages to its position.

The village of Buffalo was located at the eastern end of Lake Erie at the mouth of Buffalo Creek. This made the area safer from British attack than Black Rock, which was located along the Niagara River. The only drawback to making Buffalo the terminus was the fact that larger ships would have a harder time getting into the harbor because of the positioning of a natural sand bar across Buffalo Creek. They were forced to anchor offshore and move their cargo to smaller ships to bring the goods to shore.

The village of Black Rock was just two miles north of Buffalo on the Niagara River. It had a small natural harbor which protected it against frequent storms that occurred on the lake but sailing ships could not sail through to Lake Erie because of the Niagara River's strong currents in the opposite direction.

As usual, the simple advantages and disadvantages of both villages were clouded by political posturing. Peter Porter, an attorney from Connecticut who had purchased land along the Niagara River in the late 1700s, started a transportation business with his brothers, which handled a good deal of the trade in the upper Great Lakes. He favored the Black Rock village as the western terminus of the canal. Then he purchased more land along the Niagara River and was instrumental in building up Black Rock and supported the upgrade of the harbor to make it most advantageous. Porter furthered his influence by getting elected to the United States House of Representatives in 1809 and then served on the Erie Canal Commission from 1810 to 1816. During the War of 1812, he served as assistant quartermaster general in the New York State militia. From 1815 to 1816, he served as Secretary of State of New York; and in 1828, Porter then served as the US Secretary of War under President John Quincy Adams. He used his political brawn to help enact legislation that would enable the financial efforts to build the canal to end in Black Rock.

On the other side of the discussion were the proponents of the village of Buffalo as the western terminus. Governor DeWitt Clinton of the state of New York, also a member of the Erie Canal Commission, felt that the village of Buffalo would serve well as the terminus. Another Buffalo booster was Joseph Ellicott, the sales agent for the Holland Land Company, which owned much of the land in Western New York. Of course, his interests were led by the fact that land values in the area would sharply increase with the addition of the canal ending in Buffalo. Finally one of the early settlers in Buffalo, Samuel Wilkeson, spent a great deal of his time and talent working to make Buffalo the western terminus of the Erie Canal. His background as a merchant, politician, and judge gave him access and influence to help build up the Buffalo harbor. He supervised the dredging of the sandbar across Buffalo Creek and fought for the funds to build up the harbor to accommodate the larger ships traveling the Great Lakes.

As the canal was completed in the east and was approaching the western end, time was getting short to make a final decision. Would Black Rock serve as the western terminus of the Erie Canal or would Buffalo? Both sides hired separate engineers who would survey each harbor and come to the conclusion as to which harbor would be best. Of course, each side's engineer would side with the location that hired him. The ultimate decision would be made by canal engineers who had designed the whole expanse from Albany over the years, even though both villages had built up their own harbor sufficiently. In the end, the village of Buffalo won the day.

Even though the decisions made in the course of building the Erie Canal were made by perhaps hundreds of lawmakers, economists, commissioners, and engineers, the name most associated with this enterprise that would rival any other engineering feat in America at that time was New York governor DeWitt Clinton. His presence was felt in any and all decisions that went into the project from beginning to end. There were accolades awarded to him for his work, but there were also times when problems and issues would arise for which he took the full blame. During those times, the project would be referred to as "Clinton's Ditch" or "Clinton's Folly." Even so, the Erie Canal would ultimately be remembered as being the single most significant construction that would open the interior of New York State to commerce with the wealth and new ideas of New York and Albany.

After the decision was made and the canal was completed in Buffalo Harbor, a most prestigious person was slated to visit the completion of the construction. The Marquis de LaFayette, French aristocrat and military officer who assisted George Washington during the Revolutionary War, was making a tour of the colonies and included Buffalo as one of his stops. President James Monroe invited him to visit in part to celebrate the fiftieth anniversary of our country. He arrived in Buffalo on Saturday, June 4, 1825 and was taken to the Eagle Tavern located on the west side of Main St. near Court St., where a huge platform had been built for him and his accompanying dignitaries to stand and welcome the crowd that had been building up to thousands of people in the days previous. Lafayette was presented to the people by General Peter Porter of Black Rock, and a public reception followed. One of the dignitaries who shook Lafayette's hand on the platform was none other than the great Seneca Indian chief Red Jacket, whom Lafayette met forty years previously during the Revolutionary War. The next morning, on June 5, 1825, Lafayette was shown the impressive Erie Canal in its completed form. He then continued his tour to Black Rock, Tonawanda, and Niagara Falls (www.buffaloah.com).

The hangings of the three Thayer brothers occurred just twelve days later. Some of the crowd that had gathered for the appearance of Lafayette stayed in town for the hangings as it had been touted by authorities as an event not to be missed. Some newspapers alleged that as many as twenty thousand people were there to witness the spectacle.

Throughout the following story, I have used the real names of the people involved and, in many cases, the exact language used during the trial. It is a cautionary tale of greed, murder, and deceit perpetrated by desperate men in a time during our country's infancy when farming communities were on the edge of poverty and men's futuristic visions existed side by side.

I have written this story from the point of view of Dr. Daniel Ingalls from the Town of Concord, who performed the autopsy on John Love's body when it was found. No one can really know how the early nineteenth-century townspeople felt about a murdered body being found in their town, but by giving a voice to one who was there, we can try to understand how it must have felt.

Chapter 1

I daresay that for most of us, life will never be the same. The events of the last year are beyond what anyone's imaginings could invent. The murder itself was heinous and grotesque and would not leave my memory for quite some time. I fear many sleepless nights will be in my future as there will be for most of the kind and gentle people in this valley. Above that, the Thayer men's families will be hardest hit. They have suffered the saddest of earthly sorrows, the death of their sons, husbands, and fathers.

I suppose that as time marches on, life in these troubled times will experience many highs and lows; the struggle to survive can only be offset by the future occurrences of commerce brought to us by the new canal. I'll be able to tend to the sick and injured with new medicines brought to us from the east, and the farmers of this valley will be able to tend to their crops in more efficient ways and then sell their harvests to a wider array of buyers.

I wonder which event will be remembered the most in the year of our Lord 1825—the opening of the great Erie Canal, the visit to the village of Buffalo by the great friend of President George Washington's, the Marquis de Lafayette; or will it be the hangings of three desperate brothers caught up by the devil's discourse to murder another human being? I wouldn't have believed there could be so much change experienced in the past year by those of us trying to eke out our earthly journeys and raise families and grow our communities. As the wilderness opens up, will there be more death and disgrace, or will man hold his head up high and use his enterprising intellect to make life better for the living?

Please allow me to introduce myself. I am Dr. Daniel Ingalls from the village of Concord. My life with my family and my practice were turned upside down when I was requested to come to the village of Boston and hold an inquest and perform an autopsy on the body of a man discovered in a ravine, buried under logs, brush, and stones. I believed early on that my job as county coroner was a way to expand my knowledge and further my career, but I never expected that it would lead me to be a spectator of so much violence—so much shame—and the fact that my testimony in a murder trial would affect so many citizens.

Old Man Israel Thayer was released from custody the same day his three sons paid the ultimate price for their cruel intentions toward another human being. It would have been heinous enough for just one of them to murder another man, but all three brothers had a hand in it. All three of them were taken up by the same licentiousness, immorality, and disregard for God's own creation. What must their upbringing have been like? Were they not taught to respect others and that life, any life, was precious and needed to be protected?

This event affected four families—the parents of the boys and all three boys' wives and their children. Did they not think about how their actions would affect them? There is no liniment for a family torn apart. I've spoken to people who have seen Old Man Thayer recently, and they say that there is no light in his eyes. They're dull and empty. He has to try to pick up the pieces of the lives of his daughters-in-law and his grandchildren. As a doctor, there are times when all the study and medicines cannot help a man with a broken spirit. For so much loss suffered, only immeasurable time can heal the wounds.

It will be hard for the townspeople to be supportive of the family; their lives have been adversely affected as well. But perhaps there will be some who will, through their belief in God, help the families out to make sure they at least have enough to eat. The women will have to start working in the fields in addition to their daily duties of caring for the children, cooking, sewing, canning for the winter, churning butter, etc. Money for hardworking people was scarce. I'll give those boys one thing, when I heard that Isaac, the youngest, fraudulently took over collecting on Love's debts when he disappeared by drawing up a false affidavit and using it as "proof" that Love had asked him to do so in his absence, I was astonished. I didn't even think he could write. But seriously, I saw the document at the trial, and it wasn't the most literate and authentic piece of work I'd ever seen. The misspellings of the word "Affidavit" and "Attorney" would have been my first clue that something wasn't right. But I suppose in that crazed mind of his, falsifying an affidavit was just another way of wresting more gain from the horrible deed he and his brothers wrought.

It is summer now, and the townsfolk have to continue in their way of life as before. The planting that was done in May is growing, farmers are still tending to their animals and chores, women are still teaching their girls to cook and sew, and I am getting back to the practice of tending to people who have broken a bone or are sick in bed with some malady or other.

But the past is still hanging on in my ever-exploring mind…

Chapter 2

JOHN LOVE AND THE THAYERS

Boston is a farming community, much like Concord, New York, my hometown. The people are struggling, but it was their choice to move away from the homes they grew up in, to a new place which they could mold and work to make their own. They are courageous people and God-fearing. A member of the clergy makes a circuit around the surrounding villages, visiting and leading people in the ways of Christ.

In my community, which is just over the hill from Boston, the farms are spread far apart in such a way that children are schooled at home. In Boston, which is a larger village than Concord, there are at least three schools that the children walk to or are taken to by wagon in the winter. There is talk of expanding the school system so more children can attend and be taught by a schoolteacher.

My story involves one man, an outsider, and his relationship with a family of farmers called the Thayers. Now the Thayers, who bought the property in Boston four or five years previous, consisted of a man and his wife and their three young sons. You see, the three sons were considered ne'er-do-wells, even though they had reached the age of manhood by 1824 and were moved away from the family's farm of forty-eight acres. Their slovenly work ethic made it necessary to have other people help out the family. So they have a thirteen-year-old orphan girl by the name of Laura Willson staying with them and employ a young boy of eleven years of age by the name of Daniel Pierce to help with the farmwork.

The eldest Thayer brother, Nelson, lives perhaps a mile away to the south, and his younger brother Isaac boards with him. Nelson has a wife and some small children. The middle brother, Israel Jr., also has his own cabin about a mile north of his father's farm in which he resides with his wife and children. They were expected to help the father with his crops and his animals as they tried to make a living by selling their crops in the surrounding villages and the village of Buffalo. There was no grist mill in Boston; the closest one was in Buffalo. So the wheat had to be harvested and then taken to Buffalo to be ground into flour.

These three boys (men) were known as the village hoodlums and were particularly partial to drinking alcohol when they were bored or just didn't have a chore to do right then. The area school-master was heard to say when they were in school that they were not noted for devotion to their books. They were even proud of their surly reputation. In fact, there was a story that one day, they left together for a trip into Buffalo to try to sell a load of lumber, and they allegedly were drunk before they even started. It was a long trip into Buffalo, a good seven hours, considering they were leading oxen to carry the heavy wagon. People passing them on the road could hear them swearing at the oxen, calling them "Jesus Christ" and "God Almighty." And they must have raided their wives' trous-seau because all three were wearing bonnets instead of hats. This was not a good way to endear yourself to your community.

They were said to have worked occasionally at the only sawmill in Boston at the bottom of the hill where they lived, but I guessed that they would tire of that easily. They seemed to use the mill as their personal home away from home as they were usually found sitting on a chair in the shade, imbibing during working hours.

I asked around to find out more about the family—Old Man Thayer and his wife were much older than I thought they might be. There was a rumor that the family had come from somewhere in

Massachusetts and had left behind three older sisters to the boys, who themselves were married and still lived in Massachusetts. So Old Israel brought his three sons to the village of Boston and left behind the older siblings who, for reasons unknown, did not come with him and his wife.

Perhaps the family was fleeing for some reason; perhaps they just wanted to try to make a better life for the younger boys. Considering the boys' reputation after living in Boston for several years, they didn't seem too inclined to improve their situation.

John Love was known as a trader on the Great Lakes delivering tea, coffee, nails, molasses, salt, and furniture from the east all the way to the land around Lake Superior, where new landowners were opening up the land and homesteading. In return, these new land-owners were clearing forests and reducing the trees to potash to be shipped back to Buffalo to make soap in the factories. The lake trade was the only way to ship goods back and forth. There were no roads to the west; what few roads there were, were filled with holes and stumps. It would take weeks to take a wagonload over land, sharply increasing the price of the goods until it was no longer profitable.

Love was hired to work on a sloop called the Ohio, owned by twenty-year-old Joseph Bennett from the Town of Evans. In the winter, the lake froze over, postponing any more transporting of goods until the spring thaw. Bennett went back to Evans in the winter to be with his family, where I heard he also taught school. But Love didn't have any family; at least no one knew of any family in the area. In the summer while awaiting the sloop to be hired to ship goods west, he would stay at local rooming houses.

Apparently, he had met some citizens of Boston while doing some trading in Buffalo in the fall time and was induced into coming to Boston to spend the winter. I don't know how he ended up boarding with the neighborhood hoodlums. Perhaps he thought he could help them out monetarily as their futures seemed uncertain. Or just maybe, he saw an opportunity to lend money, which he knew wouldn't be repaid and, in the end, become a landowner when they defaulted on the loan.

He was a small man, but his life on the lakes in the summer built his body and stamina to make him imposing to any who might want to pick a fight. He spoke with an accent reminiscent of the old country across the Atlantic Ocean. He was a good dresser, wearing the clothes of a gentleman in the city. He rode a good colt and kept him brushed to a shine. He was respected by most, but he was feared by some who would stand to lose their farm or their crops if they couldn't pay him back the money they borrowed from him to keep food on their table. To look on the bright side though, he instilled in those people a better work ethic if they didn't want to lose something they had worked for, for years.

Knowing now what happened when providence brought the four of them together, I wonder if their paths might have been altered so as to keep the travesty from happening in the first place.

Chapter 3

J OHN L OVE ' S F UNERAL

It was not long after I had performed the autopsy on the alleged John Love in February 1825, when the town supervisor, John Twining, called an emergency town meeting. Most of the men who were in the search party for Love were there. I attended the meeting also in the hopes of finding out more about the unfortunate fellow. The subject of the meeting was to try to make a decision on what to do with Love's remains. Everyone was talking amongst themselves with great gusto as Eurastice Hatch placed more logs in the fire in the meeting house to heat the frigid air in the room. The body heat of the large crowd would warm the room eventually, but the fire was needed now to make our bodies stop shivering. The buzz in the air came to an abrupt halt as the supervisor's gavel crashed three times onto the block, signaling the beginning of the meeting.

"Now," said Twining, "we are here, away from our warm homes and kin, to talk about what we shall do with the decedent's remains. Most of us knew John, but we really know nothing about him personally or where his family might be. Now did anyone have any conversations with him about his past? Where is his family? What did he do before he came to Boston?"

Sylvester Irish raised his hand and stood up. "Well, I know he didn't sound like anyone around here. He had that accent that sounded British or Welsh."

"He weren't no Welsh!" spat a man in the front of the room. "My uncle's Welsh, and John didn't sound like his way of speakin'."

"Well, I didn't mean nothin' by it, you old coot, I just meant he sounded like he was from somewhere around England or such!"

"I'm just sayin'," retorted the man.

Benjamin Dole stood up and stated that he had a conversation with John last Thanksgiving about his plans on going to see his sister and mother in the spring.

"Well, where are his sister and mother?" asked the supervisor.

"He said something about 'County Kill-Kenny.' I remembered it because I have a cousin, Kenny, and it sounded like someone was going to do harm to him!"

Nervous laughter filled the room as Mr. Dole sheepishly sat back down.

"I believe that's in Ireland," said Twining.

"We'd never find his kin before his body is full of maggots and flies," said someone.

"Maybe they're livin' in this country?" said another.

"No, he told me he was going to have to book passage on a steamship," added Dole.

"Well, that's no help then, is it?" realized Twining.

There was an uncomfortable silence as the reality hit home that we weren't going to be able to find his family.

"So what are we to do then?" asked James Ives. "We've never had to deal with the death of someone with no kin."

"I didn't like him anyway," said a very tall man in the middle of the crowd. "He took a third of my fall crop and sold it in Buffalo. I think we should just take him to Potter's Field up on Fillmore Street in Buffalo and leave him. He didn't do me no favors."

"That's not true! You borrowed that $20 from him for your tax bill, and you didn't pay him back!" said a man toward the front.

"I just needed more time. I would've taken it to town and sold it anyway to pay him off, but he just took my wagon and sold it himself!"

"Perhaps you didn't like him," said someone else in the room, "but he helped me out of a bind once or twice."

"It was three times, Jacob," murmured the man sitting next to him.

Jacob threw him a nasty look and continued, "When I needed to pay James Ives for seed and didn't have any coins to pay him, John lent it to me. I paid him back right away. I thought he was a fair man."

"Well, I don't know about fair and all, but he saved my skin one time," spoke another man I did not know. "When the town demanded their pound of flesh in exchange for not doin' military service, he was right there for me. My corn was just ready for harvest, and they come knockin' on my door lookin' for money right then and there. I couldn't scrape enough together to pay them, so I asked 'em for a few days till I could sell my crops. The next day, I saw Sylvester down at the sawmill, and he mentioned that Love was at the Thayers' and that he might lend me enough until I get my crop sold to pay him back. Sylvester went and asked him, and I had the money that very same day. Yessir, he surely saved my skin that day."

"Ah, you Quakers shouldn't be allowed to pay off military service anyways! It ain't patriotic!" shouted someone from the back.

A few more shouts went up on the other side of the room, and I thought a fight was going to ensue right then and there.

The supervisor, though, had a heavy gavel and brought it down on the block with a sharp bang. "Order!" he shouted just once and the hubbub ceased.

"Now we've gone off track of the problem at hand," he said, "let us get back to the subject of this meeting."

Charles Johnson stood up and spoke. I had heard that he and his brother were the first landowners in the town when it was incorporated in 1817. I was sure the men in the room wouldn't interrupt him.

"Our town has gone through a lot in the past eight years, but we've never seen a crime like murder. We're just simple farmers and law-abiding citizens here. I'd like to think that down the road, more new families will want to come here to raise their families. So I believe that the way people will see us in the future depends on how we handle this situation. We need to show that we will embrace outsiders as equals. That people can come here to live in peace, not be afraid for their lives…that one murder is not going to define us as a community. I say that it does not matter if Love was a good man or not. His life ended tragically, and if he has no kin around here, we need to step up and treat his remains as we would any of your neighbors. His body needs to be given back to the earth. As good Christians, we are tasked with making sure his remains are treated with respect and that when we see the Lord ourselves someday, he would say to us, 'Well done, thou good and faithful servant!'"

Shouts of agreement rang up from the men.

Charles continued, "Now we all knew John. Many of us here have been the recipients of his generosity and, in good faith, paid him back. I can remember many pleasant conversations with him and laughing through the night around a fire with some hard cider. He needs to be laid to rest with some dignity."

Everyone looked into their laps with the knowledge that Charles was right, and they needed to think more about what the right thing to do was.

I hadn't offered my opinion yet, so I thought this was as good a time as any. "But, Charles, he didn't own any land here. Where shall we lay him to rest?"

"Well," said Charles thoughtfully, "I think we should build a community cemetery. We don't have a church cemetery yet…we don't even have a church. But there is obviously a need to have a place where those who can't be buried on land their family own can be laid to rest and honored in the future."

"And who has the money to buy a plot of land for that?" queried Eurastus Hatch.

"As I said before, I've been thinking about this since we discovered Love's body in the ravine behind Israel's house. I have a small piece of land that is right off the trail that is too small to farm. I can section that off and donate it to the town to be used for that exact purpose," offered Charles.

The supervisor spoke, "Charles, that is an awfully generous offer you suggest. Are you sure you want to do that?"

"I think it's something that needs to be done, and the Lord has blessed me many times in my life. I'd like to do this for the future of our community."

Charles has made a very generous offer to the town that would certainly be a solution to our problem and also offers a vision of our future as a community, thought Twining. "Does anyone else have an idea or other solution to our situation?"

Silence. No one had anything to offer or suggest alleviating the town's quandary. Charles' offer did make sense. It solved the matter of what to do with Love's remains in a civilized, Christian way and showed the townspeople and those in surrounding villages that even though a heinous crime was committed here, there was a way to move forward with life, respecting the dead and planning for the future. Perhaps a church would move in some year and build next to the cemetery, cementing the Christian way of life with the Christian way of death.

Twining looked around at the faces of the men in the room. "No? No one has any other opinion or solution to the problem before us?"

Again, nothing but an uncomfortable silence.

"Then can I get a show of hands that we accept Charles' offer?" asked Twining.

Almost every man in the room enthusiastically raised his hand in affirmation of the solution, including me. Some men were reluctant; those being the ones who felt Love belonged in Potter's Field in Buffalo. Their neighbors elbowed them to raise their hand anyway. After some persuasion, some did with a few holdouts.

"Anyone opposed?"

Fred Jones' hand moved up slowly as I'm sure he thought he might be the only one. And he was.

Twining said, "Put your hand down, Fred. Majority rules."

Fred sheepishly lowered his arm and sat there with a sour look on his face.

"Thank you, Charles. Your peers accept your proposal for a community cemetery on your donated plot of land."

"We'll mark his grave so no one will forget," added Charles.

Twining slapped down the gavel to indicate that the meeting was officially over. A collective sigh of relief could be heard among most of the men there. Everyone stood up and started talking among themselves, most comments being positive. Then conversations began about horses, sick goats, and the weather. A few men gathered around Charles Johnson, some slapping him on the back, some shaking his hand. Most of the men started leaving the meeting house and found their horses and wagons standing dutifully, waiting for their owners under a thin coating of freshly fallen snow. I, however, joined the group surrounding Charles to see what they seemed to be intently talking about.

One man was saying, "But it's the middle of March, Charles. The ground is frozen…"

"True," answered Charles. "I was thinking that I would make a coffin for him. We could set it down in the place we want to lay him and cover the box with rocks to keep the wolves off of him. Then in the spring when the ground thaws out, we'll dig the hole and set him in it."

One man said, "By then most of the smell of him would be gone too."

Mr. Hatch looked at the man and said, "Well, ain't you the delicate one?"

Everyone sniggered a little at the thought.

"I'll also carve a marker for John with his date of death and anything else we want to put on it. I've got some spare wood in my shed that I can use. I'll need a group of you men here to help me clear a space, and we'll put a temporary snake fence around the outside."

John Twining was in the group and said, "Well, you've really got this all thought out, Charles! I'll help you with the clearing and the fence."

Everyone else in the group nodded their heads and assured Charles that he could count on their help. It did my heart good to see so many men lining up to help Charles in this time of need. These were good people. And Charles had given them the opportunity to show it.

After a very cold and blustery week, Charles had completed the coffin and the grave marker, and I had heard that the men had cleared a spot and collected enough rocks to cover the coffin. A decision was made and announced at the Sunday gathering that Love would be put to rest the following Wednesday.

Tuesday came and the sun tried to make an appearance amidst a few flakes of snow. Some of us transferred Love from the unheated schoolhouse, which had been closed for the two weeks after I had performed the autopsy, to the coffin Charles made and delivered it to Charles' front porch to be ready for the following day.

I arrived at Charles' home Wednesday by wagon at 9:45 a.m. under a dark dismal sky, which was foreboding a heavy snowfall later that day. The house was dark except for one lantern on the porch rail, guiding those who would be coming later. I was a little early, so I could help out with anything. On the way to the house, I passed the spot where the grave would be. I could see where the frozen vegetation had been disturbed and a temporary fence had begun. Next to the fence was a lone wagon piled high with rocks no doubt collected over time in Charles' fields.

I stepped down from the seat of my wagon and approached the house. When I got to the porch, I walked past the last vestiges of John Love's life in the pine coffin Charles had made. I tipped my hat in reverence to the man who had suffered so egregiously at the hands of whoever had committed such a hateful crime.

Charles met me at the door and greeted me with a rather upbeat "Mornin', Doc! Come in and have some hot coffee!"

I noticed he had a black armband on his left arm just like mine.

"Much obliged, Charles!" Tipping my hat to him in greeting. "I came early in case you needed any help with anything."

"No, everything's finally done. Come sit by the fire. Coffee?"

I nodded my approval of his offer, and he poured me a steaming hot cup of coffee from the stove.

I sat down by the fire and saw there was a pot of cider warming above the flames, and his wife and young children were bustling around, preparing for any guests that might stop by for the funeral. Freshly made oatmeal cookies were being taken from the stove to a platter placed on the table that was set up for company. Charles introduced me to his wife, and we exchanged greetings. Charles wasn't a rich man by anyone's definition, but if his wife and children were anything like him, his children would surely grow up with heart and compassion and be stalwarts of the community. We sat and talked for half an hour before we began to wonder if anyone else was going to come to bid farewell to the unfortunate seaman.

As Charles' family stood by silently waiting, Charles and I stepped back out to the porch. The threat of afternoon snow was trying to make an early appearance. For a short time, the flakes came down to the point where it was difficult to see a rod in front of you. Then just as quickly as it started, the flurries died back until just a few flakes were coming down. I was glad about the snow and cold. Love's body needed to remain frozen so as not to overcome the bearers who would carry the pine box to the clearing prepared for him. Winter funerals were always tricky in that flowers and cedar chips were not available, but if the weather warmed up before they could be available, the sad aroma of the dead could be stifling.

Charles had lit his pipe from the fire before we went outside, and he stood in the snow with one hand on his hip and the other on his pipe. "Well," he said, "it's startin' to look like no one else is coming."

"Let us give them a few more minutes, Charles," I said. "I am sure someone will show up."

No sooner than I had said this when we heard the clip-clop of hooves on the frozen ground. A ghostly shape was appearing among the snowflakes, and as they got closer, I saw Benjamin Sprague and his wife, their heads and knees covered with a thin layer of snow, which they brushed away as the horses brought the wagon to a stop. Ben had been in the search party that discovered Love's body, and he had mentioned to me at the town meeting that he and his wife would surely be there to see that his remains would be entered into rest in a Christian way. He helped his young wife down from the wagon, and they approached the house with greetings and salutations.

"Charles, I made some fresh bread this morning, and the children churned up some butter. May I take it inside?" Mrs. Sprague asked.

"Well, bless your heart, Marie," Charles responded. "Of course. Go on inside and my daughter, Etta, will put it on the table. You can warm yourself by the fire."

We heard more horses approach and saw three more apparition-like wagons appear. Each one held husbands, wives, and neighbors who had ridden with them. They all brought something for the table—biscuits, some stew, and pies—all generous offerings for a man people knew little about.

Once the last wagon was emptied and the Johnson family's table was overflowing with victuals, Charles announced that the time had come to say goodbye to John Love. All the men and most of the women replaced their coats and hats and went outside while Charles' wife and some of the older women stayed behind to tend to the food and the fire.

Two men to each side of the coffin took their places and lifted the box where Love now resided and took him to the clearing where he would be forever intertwined with the wonders of God's creation—the trees, the flowers, the very dirt which contained the things that were inherently life itself.

I murmured to myself, "Ashes to ashes, dust to dust."

The group walked slowly from the Johnsons' porch where the single lantern's light dimmed with each step toward the grave. The women began softly singing "Amazing Grace" as soon as their feet began moving forward. There was no other sound in the whole valley—just a beautiful, sweet song that lingered on the snowflakes drifting down and lightly touched the ground and sweetened the rocks and soil we walked on.

We arrived at the grave, whereupon the men lowered the coffin into a small concave depression in the frozen ground. The Washburn boys, I found out later, had managed to scrape out a five-foot-by-two-foot indent in the frozen dirt. Love was a very short man, you see. The group made a small, huddled circle around the box, not exactly out of reverence but in the interest of staying warm. Elbow to elbow we stood while we waited for Charles to say some words that would be appropriate. As the town did not yet have a church, Charles, ever the man wearing many hats, officiated for the people.

Charles brushed the snow off of his *Book of Common Prayer* and voiced his thanks to God for his love of the faithful and asked for his blessings on the gathered souls brought together to say goodbye to their fallen friend. But just before Charles began his speech, I heard the soft nicker of a horse, perhaps a rod down the road, and looked up. Almost beyond my vision stood a solitary cutter pulled by a straggly-looking gray mare. A young boy sat with the reins, and three young women sat behind him. I was hardly able to make out one of the young women as Sally Thayer, young Nelson's wife. I assumed the other two women may have been the wives of the other two Thayer brothers. Those women had great courage coming out on this cold snowy day to pay their respects to the man their husbands were accused of killing. Their Christian upbringing must have been strong.

Charles began, "I am the resurrection and the life, saith the Lord: he that believeth in me, though he were dead, yet shall he live: and whosoever liveth and believeth in me shall never die. I know that my Redeemer liveth, and that he shall stand at the latter day upon the earth. And though after my skin worms destroy this body, yet in my flesh shall I see God: whom I shall see for myself and mine eyes shall behold, and not another. We brought nothing into this world, and it is certain that we carry nothing out. The Lord gave, and the Lord hath taken away. Blessed be the name of the Lord."

At this point, I was hoping that Charles would not read the entirety of "The Burial of the Dead" from the book as there were so few people here, and the snow was still coming down, freezing our feet in our boots.

He continued, "Man that is born of a woman hath but a short time to live and is full of misery. He cometh up and is cut down, like a flower. He fleeth as it were a shadow: of whom may we seek to succor, but of thee, O Lord, who for our sins art justly displeased? For as much as it hath pleased Almighty God of his great mercy to take himself the soul of our dear brother here departed, we therefore commit his body to the ground, earth to earth, ashes to ashes, dust to dust. In sure and certain hope of the resurrection to eternal life, through our Lord Jesus Christ, who shall change our vile body, that it may be like unto his glorious body, according to the mighty working, whereby he is able to subdue all things to himself."

"Lord, have mercy upon us."

"Christ, have mercy upon us," enjoined the people there.

"Lord, have mercy upon us."

As Charles closed the book, he spoke as a friend and neighbor to all, "We all knew John as a shrewd but generous man. Some thought him generous but not foolish with his bounty as he did not hesitate to share the success he enjoyed with those who needed help. He came to us after working on the Great Lakes trade, sometimes fighting sea waves and bitter conditions to bring to the village of Buffalo tools, textiles, and agricultural products which would enrich and be enjoyed by many. He wore fine clothes but helped those in need without feigning superiority.

"I've been told that he was a sailor in the Great War. He must have been a brave and sturdy man and, I daresay, a war hero. His life should have been one demanding respect and good tidings. Yet his life was cut short by a coward's bullet that ended this man's generosity and heroic life. Those gathered here on this brisk and cold wintery day will hopefully remember John Love not only for who he was—a friend and a neighbor—but what he represented—a comrade in arms, a courageous man willing to fight against oppression, a fighting man not afraid to die for a cause, and a steward of the bounty he personally experienced.

"I am certain he wasn't perfect. No man is. But God doesn't demand perfect children, only those who can say they tried. Those who wake up in the morning and say, 'It's going to be a good day,' and to go about their life seeking God and his glory in everything that we do."

Then Charles led the group in The Lord's Prayer: "Our Father which art in heaven, hallowed be thy Name, thy kingdom come, thy will be done in earth as it is in heaven: Give us this day our daily bread and forgive us our trespasses, as we forgive them that trespass against us. And lead us not into temptation but deliver us from evil. Amen."

"Amen," repeated the group.

Then finally, with one hand raised high over his head, Charles finished the service for the unfortunate fellow with: "Hallelujah! Give thanks to the Lord, for he is good, for his mercy endures forever. Who can declare the mighty acts of the Lord or show forth all his praise? Happy are those who act with justice and always do what's right!"

Then he bowed his head and everyone there followed suit. "Remember me, O Lord, with the favor you have for your people and visit me with your saving help. That I may see the prosperity of your elect and be glad about the gladness of your people, that I may glory with your inheritance.

"The grace of our Lord Jesus Christ, and the love of God, and the fellowship of the Holy Ghost, be with us all evermore. Amen."

Again, hushed murmurs of "Amen" could be heard from the men and women around the circle.

The shuffling of feet was all that could be heard in the crisp air as people started getting ready to depart, hoping that their feet would warm up quickly. I stayed behind with some of the other men to see to the transfer of rocks from the wagon to the prone casket lying in the depression the Washburn boys had scraped away. The women and the other older men returned to the Johnson house. With many men working together, we moved all of the rocks and surrounded Love's remains with them in no time at all. All the physical activity warmed us up a little and dislodged the snow from our shoulders, but even so, we hurried to get back to the house.

We all waited until we got closer to the house before we took our hands out of our pockets and gloves to brush off the quickly deepening snow off our hats. It felt as if it had gotten colder than before, and our hands were reluctant to be removed from cover. Our eyelashes were also covered with crystalline stuff, giving us the appearance of frozen statues. We arrived back at the house in no time.

I looked down the trail and between the snowflakes saw Mrs. Sprague speaking to the Thayer women. I had hoped that someone would invite them to come into the house to warm up. I saw Sally Thayer shake her head and politely refuse the offer. The boy at the reins shook them onto the horses' backs, and they turned around and disappeared behind the curtain of snow.

The women had, while we were gone, prepared the table with all manner of foods provided by the families and had started portioning out the warm cider that had been hung over the coals. We piled up our coats and hats in the corner of the living area. It was a tight fit, but we all managed to arrange ourselves around the blazing fire. The heat felt wonderful.

After Mrs. Johnson said the blessing, the women served the men plates full of the food prepared for the occasion. Then once the men had been served, the women took for themselves smaller plates, and the Johnson children shared with their mother. They all sat around the perimeter of the room so as to allow the men to get the most from the hearth's warmth.

There was small talk among the women, but the men got into a discussion about what was to happen next. The Thayers had been arrested and were in the *gaol* in Buffalo, but what if they didn't do it? Was there still a murderer in our midst?

"How long do you think it'll be before there will be a trial?" queried Sylvester Irish.

Supervisor Twining thought that since the crime was one most foul, there would be a trial as soon as spring arrived. He imagined that many people in the town would be asked to testify and thought that it would be prudent to wait until the road to Buffalo was more passable.

The men nodded in agreement and asked the women if there were more cider. The pot was almost empty, but they managed to eke out a smaller portion for everyone. Then the conversation began to get lighter as we finished our meal. Many asked to be excused and reclaimed their coats and hats to brush the snow off their horses and wagons and make their way home. Handshakes were offered, and thanks were given to Charles for making this happen.

The horses, seeing everyone come outside en masse, shook their heads of the powder that had accumulated, knowing that they would be on the move soon. Brooms were brought out and places were made on the wagons for people to sit. I stayed until the last wagon had left and was grateful to see the snow tapering off although the trip home over the hill would be treacherous with all the snow that fell the last few hours. I patted my horse on the neck and told her that I was counting on her to get the cutter home. Charles, with pipe in hand, waved to me from the porch and went back inside to the warmth of his hearth and his family.

Chapter 4, Part 1

THE TRIAL

The day came for the Thayer brothers to be tried for their alleged crime. The district attorney, H. B. Potter, was holding the trial at the Court of Oyer and Terminer in the village of Buffalo before the Honorable Reuben H. Walworth, who was the judge for the Fourth Circuit Court of New York State.

I was subpoenaed to testify and bear witness to the events of February last, whereupon I performed the autopsy on John Love after the townspeople had found his body buried in a shallow grave in a ravine, covered only with logs, leaves, and stone. The story went that his stocking feet were sticking up through the snow.

It took seven hours to travel to the village, and those of us who were to testify in the morning traveled together. Dr. Emmons S. Gould, another medical examiner from the area, and I traveled in one wagon. We brought with us all the reports and drawings we had made of the autopsy to submit to the court. Frederick Jones, John Stafford, and Reuben Irish traveled in a second wagon and so on, forming quite a lengthy caravan as probably half the town of Boston was called to testify in the morning.

Our journey began at 4:00 a.m. on the morning of the twentieth of April 1825. It was a brisk and cold morning with a hint of snow in the air. We bundled ourselves with warm woolen blankets and furs and started out on our way. The first hour or so, we spent talking about what we were going to say at the trial and the anticipation of the court asking further questions of us. Preparing short statements about the direction the ball came from and went through the body in a way that would not frighten the weak of heart was difficult, not knowing how descriptive we should be. This was a situation that was entirely new to both of us, and we weren't sure what to expect. After we went over the things we wanted to say, we spent a good deal of the rest of the time in silence; the snow softly falling and the horses nodding their disapproval of the long walk in the cold. We had prepared blankets for them as well, but it seemed too little to make them happy.

Most of the men in our procession were fathers themselves, and I'm sure it had crossed the minds of many how a son of theirs might act to be in as much trouble as these boys were. I say boys, but they were all grown men with wives and children of their own. They all lived on the same hill together with separate houses, just walking distance from each other. It was not only unlawful what they did, but how could they put their families through this? After speaking to some of the townspeople, it shouldn't be a surprise to anyone that these brothers had gotten into such trouble. Ostensibly, they had a reputation for not quite being upstanding members of the community. I had learned that whenever a theft in the area occurred, they were the first to be suspected of committing the act. It was also rumored that they imbibed in the fermented juice of the grape quite often, as well as owned a still where they produced harder liquor. Their father was a farmer, but it was known that the three didn't exactly pick up any knowledge on how to grow crops for theirs failed quite often.

In my conversations with the townspeople about John Love, there were people who liked him and others who despised him. He was a small man, hardly five and a half feet tall, who apparently was born in the old country, probably Ireland or Scotland; no one knew exactly which. He had no relatives here and was only in Boston for the winter. He seemed to be flush with cash, which was extremely unusual for a small village. He made his living in the lake trade during the summer and bought and sold goods at a small profit. So when he came to town, he offered to lend money to people, sometimes using crops, sometimes using property as collateral. Many people were able to pay him back after taking their crops to Buffalo to sell, but an unfortunate few could not and thereby ceded their property to him. He was said to be very shrewd in his business dealings, although fair to some people who just needed a helping hand. He had a fine horse, and his clothing was new and well cared for. He wore fine boots that would have been the envy of even a gentleman.

The weather had been kind to us, and we reached the village of Buffalo in good time. Dr. Gould and I stopped at a tavern for a meal and to make arrangements for an overnight stay. I was requested to be at the courthouse no later than eight the next morning, so we found a place that was close by. The others in our procession did the same. I discovered later that the tavern keepers thought it strange that so many people from the same town were looking for lodging at the same time, and they weren't suitably prepared. My companion and I had to share a cold room with six others, and there were no beds provided, just a mat of hay on the floor for us to place our bedrolls. The food situation was far from optimal as they weren't expecting so many people at one time. The meals only consisted of some pan-fried pork and some rather overbaked bread. Our horses and buckboards were cared for by the hostlers in the wagon yard. I could only hope that they were fed sufficiently for our trip back home.

We walked to the courthouse the following morning as the sun shone brightly in the sky and illuminated the village's downtown section. Neither of us had been there before, and we were taken with the size and scope of some of the buildings. The courthouse itself was impressive with its shining granite front and large windows centered with a heavy wooden door on great iron hinges. There were many people milling around outside, but I wanted to get inside and claim a good seat for myself and my fellow physician.

We were led into the courtroom by an attendant who was to place us in an area reserved for those testifying at the trial. There was a small grouping of chairs arranged for spectators. The walls consisted of dark ominous mahogany paneling. The judge's bench, situated higher than the rest of the room, was enclosed in the same paneling and exuded an air of superiority, which I suppose it must. It was, nonetheless, very impressive. On the wall behind the judge's chair was the great seal of New York State, flanked by the American flag and the flag of New York State. The jury box to the left held twelve heavy walnut chairs where the twelve men would sit and listen to the testimony of all the witnesses and the oratories of the district attorney and the lawyers for the defense and the lawyers for the prosecution and decide the fate of the three men who were accused of the horrid crime. We took seats on the left side of the room, in front of the juror's stand, and awaited the time to come for things to get started.

The brothers had already been arraigned on an indictment consisting of four counts including assault, discharge of a gun, and murder. Surprisingly, they pled "Not guilty." Their father, Israel Thayer Sr., was also charged with aiding his sons in committing the crime, but he would not be on trial today. Usually, the courts would perform a separate trial for each person accused of the same crime, but Israel Jr. and Isaac's crimes were identical, and in the interest of saving the court time and money, they would be tried together. The elder brother Nelson's crimes were slightly different in that it was determined that he cast the deadly blow with an axe, so his trial was scheduled after Isaac and Israel's.

The room filled up, and the echo of voices rang in the room until one could hardly have a conversation with one's neighbor without raising one's voice. Finally after a good quarter of an hour, the bailiff walked into the room from the judge's chambers and asked everyone to stand while the judge came in and took his seat.

The room became quieter while the bailiff announced, "The Honorable Reuben H. Walworth, judge for the Fourth Circuit Court of New York State."

The room became hushed as the clerk read off the crimes that the brothers were being charged with: "That Israel Thayer Jr.—late of the Town of Boston, in the County of Erie, laborer—and Isaac Thayer— late of the said Town of Boston, in said county, laborer—not having the fear of God before their eyes but being moved and seduced by the instigation of the devil on the fifteenth day of December in the year of our Lord one thousand eight hundred and twenty-four, with force and arms at the said Town of Boston in the county aforesaid, in and upon one 'John Love' in the peace of God and of the said people then and there being feloniously, willfully, and with malice aforethought did make an assault, and that they, the said Israel Thayer Jr. and Isaac Thayer, a certain gun called a rifle of the value of $10, then and there loaded and charged with gunpowder and one leaden bullet, which said gun, they, the said Israel Thayer Jr. and Isaac Thayer, in both their hands then and there, had and held, then and there feloniously, willfully and with malice aforethought, did shoot off and discharge at, against and upon the said John Love, and that they, the said Israel Thayer, Jr. and Isaac Thayer, with the leaden bullet aforesaid out of the gun aforesaid, then and there by force of the gunpowder aforesaid, the said Israel Thayer Jr. and Isaac Thayer, discharged and sent forth as aforesaid then and there feloniously, willfully and with their malice aforethought did strike, penetrate, and wound the said John Love near the outer angle of the right eye of him, the said John Love, then and there with the leaden bullet aforesaid shot, discharged and sent forth out of the gun aforesaid by them, the said Israel Thayer Jr. and Isaac Thayer, in manner aforesaid, one mortal wound penetrating in and through the head of him, the said John Love, of which said mortal wound the said John Love then and there instantly died."

I leaned closer to my friend, Dr. Gould, and said, "If the length of the clerk's report of the charges is an indication of how long this trial will proceed, I fear we may miss the delights of the spring and summer as it passes us by!"

Mr. Gould smiled and nodded his agreement.

Then continuing, the clerk read the indictment against the boys' father, "And that one Israel Thayer, late of the Town of Boston in the county aforesaid, laborer, otherwise called Israel Thayer Sr., not having the fear of God before his eyes, but being seduced by the instigation of the devil, before the felony and murder aforesaid by the aforesaid Israel Thayer Jr. and Isaac Thayer, in the manner and form aforesaid was done and committed. That is to say on the fifteenth day of December in the year aforesaid, with force and arms at the said Town of Boston in the county aforesaid, did maliciously, feloniously, voluntarily, and of his malice aforethought, incite, stir up, move, procure, aid abet counsel, and command the said Israel

Thayer Jr. and Isaac Thayer, to do and commit the felony and murder aforesaid, in the manner and form aforesaid, against the peace of the people of the state of New York and their dignity."

The district attorney, H. B. Potter, got up and addressed the accused's attorneys—Thomas C. Love (no relation to the decedent), E. Griffin, and E. B. Allen, Esq.—and stated that since Israel Thayer Jr.'s and Isaac Thayer's crimes were identical in nature and performance, the court asked them whether they objected to the two of them being tried together. Their consent was given, and the clerk proceeded to call the jury to the stand. As they came into the room, the jury was sworn in by the clerk: Mr. James Clark, Mr. Thomas Decker, Mr. Reuben Rogers, Mr. George Blackman, Mr. J. P. Morey, Mr. Samuel Slade, Mr. Ornith Manfield, Mr. Levi Evans, Mr. Michael Dunn, Mr. Everett Knight, Mr. R. D. Crego, and Mr. Josiah Brown.

Mr. Potter got up and addressed the jury with their instructions for their time in court. He was a tall man, very stately, and fine. He was wearing a smart, tailored woolen suit that showed his status in the legal world.

"The cause now to be submitted to you is the most important that can occur in human jurisprudence, a cause which requires the exercise of all your candor and intelligence. It has fallen to your lot to sit in judgment upon the lives of two of your fellow men. The prisoners stand indicted for the murder of John Love, have pleaded 'not guilty,' and have put themselves upon their country which country you are. The crime charged is one of the deepest die, the most abhorrent and revolting to our nature. It equally shocks the feelings of the civilized man and the savage.

"We find in every human breast the same horror of the crime— the same dread and detestation of the perpetrators. The crime has been known from the beginning—it is to be heard of in our first records—we are not to look for its history in our statute books alone. It is to be found on every page of the history of man.

"But for its punishment, we look to the laws of the land, the laws of nature, and the laws of God. It equally contravenes them all and all equally denounce the crime and declare the penalty. 'Thou shalt not kill' is a law announced by the great lawgiver of the universe to which nature and human reason and the wisdom of ages have responded assent.

"An essential ingredient of the crime of murder is malice or the intention of killing. Malice is either expressed or implied. With the latter, we have little to do, or with the implication of law in particular cases of homicide. Every killing of a human being is not to be accounted a murder. Malice aforethought, or a determination to kill, is essential to constitute this crime. Judge Blackstone[1] defines murder to be 'the unlawful killing of any reasonable creature in the king's peace with malice aforethought by a person of sound memory.'

"Express malice is now the grand criterion which distinguishes 'murder' from other killing. It is defined to be a sedate deliberate determination of the mind and a formed idea to do the injury, which is formed by evidence such as lying in wait, previous menaces, former grudges, and definitive schemes. From these definitions, I find no difficulty as to the evidence of express malice in the case before you. As to John Love's death, it will be shown to have been *most awfully* and *too successfully* premeditated. We will discover next by whom the crime was perpetrated—that it was done by the prisoners or that they were instrumental in it. For if more than one person is involved, it is no matter if one gave the fatal blow or discharged the fatal bullet. They were all present aiding, abetting, or assisting in the act. The law in such a case makes them all principles. This trial will involve an examination of a long and tedious string of circumstances. And to this investigation, I must invite your particular attention and solicit the fullest exercise of your patience.

"When crimes are so flagrant and so universally abhorrent as the one charged here, witnesses to the fact are not often called upon. The murderer hides his head from humanity and the light. The deed is done in darkness and in private. The intention is to evade discovery—to keep the deed in darkness, where there is no human ear to hear nor eye to detect nor human arm to stay the fatal blow. Such was

---

[1] Sir William Blackstone was an English jurist, judge, and Tory politician of the eighteenth century. He is most noted for writing the *Commentaries on the Laws of England.*

the case of the murderers of John Love. There was no suicide as will clearly appear from the testimony. But whether murdered during the day or the night, the foul deed is enveloped in midnight darkness.

"I expect to prove such a train of circumstances such a connected chain of facts, perfect in every link, as to remove from your minds every reasonable doubt—and possibly every vestige of skepticism—that the prisoners are the murderers. If you find satisfactory evidence of the prisoners' guilt, you are bound to act, and I trust will independently decide them to be guilty."

At that time, Mr. Potter quoted a law that, honestly, was beyond my ability to understand; he spoke it very quickly, and I couldn't keep up. I believe it had something to do with a definition of the word "proof."

That being explained to the jurors, he continued with his instructions, "If they are guilty, you must so find them. If so, they are unfit for human society. It will be urged to you that there exists great excitement in the public mind against the prisoners. There is excitement undoubtedly. But that there is or has been undue excitement on this occasion, I deny. On the announcement of so flagrant a murder as appears here to have been perpetrated, is it strange that excitement should prevail? The whole community ought at once to arm and turn out for the discovery of the felons. The alacrity and vigilance of the people of Boston are evidence that their moral sense still exists and that virtue still prevails amongst them. With such people, your life and property may be considered safe. But prejudice or excitement cannot alter guilt or innocence. Truth is and will be the same."

The district attorney completed his opening arguments (thank the heavens for small favors!) with this admonishment—that truth cannot be hidden or changed through prejudice or excitement.

I was the first of many persons who were called to testify on this initial day of the trial.

The clerk called my name out loud and with great authority, "Dr. Daniel Ingalls, physician. Approach the witness stand to be sworn to truthfulness before God and this assembly."

I took my leave from the side of my companion and fellow physician and snaked my way around other spectators seated around us. The room took on a profound silence so that every footstep seemed to echo like thunder within it. I reached the witness stand and turned to face the clerk, who, after telling me to place my left hand on top of the Bible he held in his hand, entreated me to raise my right hand and swear to all those learned attorneys, the honorable judge, and the simplest of farmers in attendance, that I promised to tell the truth, the whole truth, and nothing but the truth, so help me God. After assenting my agreement, I was told to be seated, and Atty. Sheldon Smith for the People began his questions of me.

"Dr. Ingalls, please tell us how you came to be called to the Town of Boston to act as county coroner after the discovery of the body of John Love."

"On February the twenty-fourth last, my presence was requested through a courier by the constable in that town. I was requested to hold an inquest to examine the body of a man who had been found buried behind a home owned by Israel Thayer Jr."

"And if you please, can you share with us the results of that inquest?" requested Mr. Smith.

"On examination of the body, there appeared to be a ball hole entirely made through the head on one side and out the other."

Several of the women gasped at such a description, but I had to continue. It would only get more gruesome as I continued.

"The hole was above the cheekbone near the outer angle of the eye. I passed a probe through the head and met no obstruction except for fragments of bone. The ball passed near but below the brain. I do not believe that it would have produced instant death. He might have lived a few hours, perhaps days. If the brain had been injured, instant death would not necessarily ensue, but it most likely would have.

"The hole was the smallest on the right side, and I concluded that the ball had entered on that side. There was another wound on the back of the head near the crown or vertex that fractured the skull bone. It caused a fracture from the top to the bottom of the head and appeared to have been done with the head of an axe."

Yet more gasps from the spectators were heard. Some women even excused themselves to the door outside, where they did not have to listen further.

After giving time for the exodus to stop, I continued, "The bone could be pressed inwardly and, on removing the pressure, would regain its place by the elasticity of the brain. The skin was also broken and the flesh apparently much bruised. The fracture was about two inches long and one or one-half inches wide. The effect of this would be to induce stupor and probably would terminate in death. It probably affected the brain. From its situation, it would compress the brain.

"There was another bruise behind the left ear, on the thick part of the temporal bone. I believe that it would have been produced with the same instrument as the other, most probably the head of an axe. The skin was broken and flesh bruised. The bone was not fractured in this spot behind the left ear. It would require a hard blow to produce death in that place. It might produce concussion if hard enough. I could not tell decisively the full effect of this blow.

"There was yet another wound across the face or cheek extending down to the windpipe. I cannot conclude whether it was cut or torn off. Part of the cheek was cut down to the bone but not cut off entirely. The flesh on the upper and lower jaws was partly cut off so as to leave the bone bare on both jaws. The neck appeared to be broken. The two bones forming the bridge of the nose were broken down and flattened down entirely. The vertebra, or ligaments, appeared to be separated. The body appeared to have been partly frozen, especially the feet and fingers."

Mr. Smith, not apparently fazed with the gruesome details I had just explained, asked me to sum up my findings.

"I was satisfied that the neck was broken, but I cannot say where—whether near the head or lower down. The effect of the dislocation of the neck would be instant death or not, according to the manner of the injury. There are examples in the books where death did not instantly ensue upon a dislocation. It depends upon the injury done to the spinal marrow. Most probably, though, it would have produced instant death. If not death, it would have produced a paralysis of all the lower extremities inevitably. The wound on the face extended down under the chin into and across the windpipe. It appeared there to have been cut by a sharp instrument, like an axe. I do not know whether one or two blows produced the wound. An axe might do it by one blow, I think, if the stroke was a glancing one."

Mr. Smith, attorney for the state, thanked me for my testimony and expertise in the human anatomy, and next, I was to be questioned by Atty. E. Griffin, counsel for the prisoners. Mr. Griffin was a gruff, hardened-looking man, wearing a suit of questionable tailoring and obviously one or two sizes too big. Either that or he had recently lost some weight. His mammoth imperial mustache was so long it fluttered as the words escaped from his barrel-chested lungs and deep voice box.

He coughed and stuttered a little as he began questioning me, "Dr. Ingalls, what—uh, what sort of gun would you say the ball came from that entered the back of Mr. Love's head?"

"As I am a physician, sir, and not a gun expert, I cannot determine whether the ball came from a pistol, a musket, or a rifle," I said.

"And what of the wound, uh, on the back of the head? Can you be more precise as to the weapon that was used that would have caused such a wound?" returned the counselor.

"Again, sir, I can form no precise idea of the instrument that produced the wound. I believe it would have been an iron instrument, most likely an axe," I said.

Mr. Griffin looked decidedly miffed at my answers so far, but he continued, "Dr. Ingalls, did you determine that, uh, (cough) the cheekbone was fractured?"

"No, sir, I don't believe the cheekbone was fractured. The flesh was just torn away from it," I answered.

"You have testified, sir, that a glancing stroke of an axe might have given the wound on the face and neck, is that correct?"

"Yes, sir, if the blow had been given with a sword or such a kind of instrument, it would have been a most powerful blow. I cannot say from the angles of the wound that it was possibly made by a sword or other springing instrument. It was across the face and chin, and the jawbone was very apparently dislocated. The integuments had given way and were injured," I continued.

"Dr. Ingalls, sir, uh, pardon my ignorance, but uh, integuments?"

"My apologies, sir. Integuments are the skin and flesh that hold the jawbone and nose cartilage together," I explained.

"All right then, please continue," he requested.

"Well, sir, I was just about to say that whether the instrument was an axe or a sword, the blow would have been a glancing one with the ability to carry off part of the cheekbone, depending on the direction of it."

Mr. Griffin turned to face the judge, took a breath to say something, decided not to, thanked me for my testimony, and quietly walked back to his seat at the prisoners' table.

Mr. Smith arose from his chair and asked the judge if he could be allowed to redirect more questions to me. The judge nodded his permission, and he approached me once again.

"Dr. Ingalls, if you please tell the jury your first impressions of the body when you approached it for the first time in the schoolhouse in North Boston?" he asked.

"The body of the deceased was a male, about five and a half feet tall, and must have been dead some considerable time. Putrefaction had commenced and had proceeded so far that the body was very disagreeable. Those in attendance all had covered their noses and mouths with their kerchief so as to avoid breathing the malicious odor.

"The winter had been quite open and rather warm, though there had been some snow. I could not form a judgment as to the length of time the man had been dead. It could have been four, eight, or even ten weeks. It depends materially upon circumstances connected with life, habits, manner of death, and burial," I continued.

"Yes, yes. I'm sure it was difficult to determine how long the deceased had been lying in the ground," Mr. Smith interrupted. "Were there any other injuries to the body?"

Perplexed by the bard's seeming agitation, I offered slowly, "Beyond the description I have already attested to, I discovered no other wounds on the body."

He looked at the judge and said, "I have no further questions."

With that being said, the judge excused me, and I took my seat in the gallery. I was well satisfied with my testimony, although, I must say, I did not understand Atty. Smith's impatience. I was merely expressing the factors involved in determining how long a man might have been dead and lying unprotected from the elements. Before I could think any further on the subject, the clerk called out for my companion, Dr. Gould, to take the witness stand.

Mr. Smith stood again and approached him after the clerk swore him into his truthfulness.

"Dr. Gould, please tell us your occupation and what you perceived at the coroner's inquest regarding the death of John Love?" he asked.

"Well, I am a medical doctor practicing in the Town of Boston, and Dr. Ingalls and I were called to give our expert opinion on the status of a body, thought to be that of one John Love that the townspeople had discovered after he had gone missing for nigh unto two months. We inspected the body together. The wound through the head appeared to have been made by a ball, which entered on the right side below the angle of the eye and came out close to the outer angle of the left eye. Some part of the right eye was left in the head. The left eye was so injured that it had almost wholly decayed. The ball passed so near as almost to cut the angle of the eye. The hole was forward of and under the brain. The size of the ball hole depends on the distance from the gun that caused it. And the state of the body at the time of the examination might essentially alter the appearance of the wound. I judged the ball had entered the right side because the integuments, sorry, the skin and flesh were carried in on that side. On the other side, on the left side of his face, the skin and flesh appeared to be protruding. A rifle ball in its whirling course must make a larger wound than that of a musket."

"Dr. Gould, can you focus on your findings of the wounds caused by a sharp instrument such as an axe?" Mr. Smith asked.

"Certainly. The wound on the face was on the right cheek, nearly from the nose to the ear. The center of the wound was the highest on the cheekbone nearly up to the eye. And the extremities of the wound were about equal in height. The flesh on the cheek and part of the upper and part of the lower lip were laid down, and the muscles had contracted so as to exaggerate the appearance of the size of the wound. In passing down, the instrument appeared to have injured the bone, which appears to be fractured, and the lower jaw was dislocated. I am confident that this was so, as the integ—sorry, the skin and flesh had given away," Emmons continued. "The wound extended under the chin into the neck, and the windpipe was nearly separated. It extended so far down as necessarily to separate some of the arteries, but the whole wound might not occasion instant death.

"On the back of the head, or nearly on the back, the wound was about two inches or two and a half inches in length and half an inch in width. The skin and flesh were gone. The skull bone was bare and fractured through the whole size of the wound. It was shivered into five or six pieces. The effect might have been death without immediate relief. It would depend on the degree of the concussion and the energy of his system to heal. I could not determine whether without aid he would have recovered. The wound under the left ear was upon the hard bone. The skin was broken, and the flesh was bruised. But I could not discover if the bone was broken. It would require a hard blow to fracture that bone. These wounds altogether would certainly have produced instant death. The neck was dislocated at the first vertebra. The cartilage connecting the joint appeared to be partly separated. There would have been a total of two blows, one on and down the cheek and another below on the neck, which would have been the blow that dislocated the neck."

Seemingly satisfied with Dr. Gould's graphic descriptions of the gruesome injuries the decedent had suffered and sensing that the jurors were becoming overcome with gastric gyrations after listening to the details, the district attorney ceased his questioning and excused Dr. Gould.

The first of the testimonies from the townspeople was Mr. Frederick T. Jones. He looked uncomfortable in the suit that was probably borrowed—farmers are used to overalls and boots, not a button-down shirt, wool trousers, and a poorly tied cravat, which seemed to be choking the very life out of a man not used to such constriction.

After adjusting the cravat and swallowing a couple of times, Mr. Jones began by saying, "I found the body the day before the coroner's inquest was held in the field on Israel Thayer Jr.'s land, about thirty rods from the house near the footpath from Israel's to Reuben Irish's place. The grave was directly on the old pathway. It had been an old road before the land was cleared when the trees that were chopped down fell across the path at that spot, so the road was no longer used. Then the path went round the trees and directly came in again."

At this point, the district attorney asked him to explain the actual discovery of the body.

"The body lay in the old path near a large log. I think the grave might be seen from the new path, especially in the winter," said Jones.

Mr. Potter interrupted him and asked him, "How did you come to look in that particular area, Mr. Jones?"

"Well, that morning, while I was summoning the people to assist in making search for the body, Mr. Britton gave me some information that induced me to search this land of Israel's particularly. One of my company soon discovered the grave. The body lay as close to the log as a grave could be dug and was short and narrow. The dirt had been drawn back from the log and thrown back to its place and made level and smooth and old chunks and pieces of wood thrown on the top. The ground was frozen over the body, so we had to dig around the middle of the body and found the great coat which I had known Love to wear. On opening the grave further, we discovered the foot of the body. It was then I knew we found Love's body, and I left the grave and went to arrest Israel Jr. and his father at Nelson Thayer's, whom I also arrested and took them to Judge Rector's."

"So you left the prisoners at the judge's and did you then return to the grave?" asked Mr. Potter.

"Yes, sir, I returned to the grave once I knew the prisoners were being detained by the judge and the men we placed as guards. On my return, the company had removed all the earth from around the body, leaving it in the position as it was found. It was then lifted and placed on a board and carried to the schoolhouse where the coroner's inquest was held."

"Was there any doubt in your mind, Mr. Jones, that the body was that of John Love?" asked the district attorney.

"Sir, I have no doubt it was the body of John Love. I have known him for about two years, and I recognized his body beyond any doubt. Also, the great coat that was found on the body was his," rejoined Mr. Jones.

Mr. Potter then asked, "Mr. Jones, is it not true that Israel Jr. had attended previous days' searches for the body?"

"Yes and I requested him to help me on this day, but he declined. He gave no reason, but when I went out to arrest him, he was standing on a bridge along the road about fifty rods from the body."

"Your witness, Mr. Griffin," bellowed the district attorney at a volume of which I was not expecting, and I am quite sure I leaped six inches off the seat of my trousers with the unexpectedness of it!

I looked around sheepishly, wondering if any had seen my embarrassing reaction, and saw that others were startled by the District Attorney's loud voice as well. As the shuffling of startled feet waned, Bard Griffin approached Constable Jones to affect more information from him.

"Mr. Jones, sir. Did you ask young Thayer why he wouldn't join the company in their search for Love?" Mr. Griffin queried.

"Um, yes, I now recollect that when I requested Israel Jr. to assist me in the search, as I before stated, he said he was going after a load of hay, and I think he did that day get a load of hay," reported Mr. Jones.

"Thank you, Mr. Jones. You may step down." Griffin was done with this witness.

John Stafford of North Boston was called next to testify. He was again sworn in and sat down at the front of the room.

"Mr. Stafford, please tell the jury what you saw as part of the search party?" asked Mr. Potter.

"I was the person who found the body first," said Stafford, "but I was not there when he was uncovered, nor did I see his face until he was taken to the schoolhouse. I saw the body again there, and I have no doubt it was Love. I also knew his clothes."

"How else were you able to recognize that it was Love?" asked Mr. Potter.

"There was a scar that I had previously known about Love's head which I also perceived on this body. Love's hair was darkish, not really inclining to be sandy. I had known Love fairly well, and I have no doubt that it was his body, God rest his soul," finished Stafford.

Mr. Griffin took his turn cross-examining Stafford.

"On my arrival near the place of the grave, I discovered that some things had been stirred—it appeared that some chunks of wood had been moved. I got on top of the large log and noticed the dirt had been moved and called out to the company that I found him. Perhaps I could have discovered the moved dirt a few feet off without getting on the log, but the place was surrounded by brush and logs. I, at first, thought that wood might have been drawn from the path by a team of mules, but when I determined that they could not get out from there, I was led to examine the area more closely when I discovered the grave," Mr. Stafford completed.

At this time during the trial, Dr. Gould and I realized that the day before us would be long and tedious. We shifted our weight in our chairs to give a rest to various parts of our seats. More people were arriving in the courtroom every few minutes, and it was becoming rather close and stifling as more people entered the spacious room, although not spacious enough when filled to capacity. The district attorney, it seemed, had subpoenaed most of the people in the whole of Boston as most residents there had known John Love or knew of him. Indeed, the room would soon become a standing room only as witnesses for the prosecution arrived to take their turn being questioned.

Reuben Irish, Nelson Thayer's neighbor, was the next witness.

Sheldon Smith, another attorney for the prosecution, began the questioning of Mr. Irish. "Mr. Irish, please tell the court where you live in proximity to the defendants."

He began, "I live about a mile from Nelson Thayer's. I'm rather farther than that from Israel Thayer's."

"And what was your experience on December fifteenth last?" continued Mr. Smith.

"I was at Nelson's house and saw Love there on the fifteenth of December. It was about sundown, and Love was holding his colt by the bridle. Mr. Washburn was also there, and Nelson was chopping wood at his door."

"And how was Love dressed?" queried Mr. Smith.

"Love had on an old gray great coat, or a sort of roundabout, and a cap on his head," said Irish.

"Was Love a native of Boston? Did he have any family there?" asked Atty. Smith.

"I don't know if Love had any family, but he had made it his home at several places in Boston over the years."

"What happened then?" asked Smith.

"John, Nelson, and his brother Isaac left there together and went toward Israel's house," said Irish. "The brothers led the way to Israel's house, and John followed them with his horse. He was a little way behind the Thayers because it had taken a minute or two to mount his horse. He soon caught up with them," said Irish.

"And had you seen Love since that day?" asked Smith.

"I hadn't seen John since that day in December. I didn't hear anybody speaking about seeing him recently, rather, folks talked about the fact that they thought he had gone away for a time," Irish answered.

"Your witness," said Mr. Smith.

Atty. Griffin, representing the accused, got up to question Mr. Irish. He began, "Mr. Irish, now in order to go from Nelson Thayer's to Israel Thayer's, you pass the sawmill, which is about fifty rods from Nelson's, is that correct?"

Reuben started, "Well, when I saw them together at Nelson's, it was nearly dark, and they had not yet reached the sawmill as far as I could see. I then went to Mr. Washburn's house with him."

Griffin interrupted him, "Didn't you tell the district attorney a different story?"

"No," said Irish, a bit taken back. "I have not at any time told a different story. I was of the impression that all three brothers left

Nelson's together. I remember the day was the fifteenth of December because that evening I settled a debt with Mr. Washburn, and we made receipts that bear that debt. I have them here with me now," he said as he started to reach in his trouser pocket.

"No, no, that won't be necessary," said Griffin. "You can step down."

Reuben stuffed the receipts back in his pocket and looked disturbed that he had been accused of lying. He shook his head and went back to his seat in the gallery.

"The court calls Mr. Samuel Washburn to the stand," announced the clerk.

Mr. Washburn left his seat and walked up to the witness stand and took a chair there that had been vacated by Mr. Irish.

Mr. Potter got up to speak, "Mr. Washburn, what are your recollections of the day in question, the fifteenth of December last?"

Sam answered him, "Well, the last I saw of Love was that day when Reuben Irish settled a debt with me—I have a receipt with the date on it. I was at Nelson Thayer's about sundown as were Nelson's two brothers. All four of them left and went toward Israel's. Nelson got before Love while he was mounting his horse."

"And what kind of coat was Love wearing?" asked Potter.

"He was wearing a gray great coat. I have seen him wear it before. It was the same one that was on the dead body at the inquest at the schoolhouse," said Washburn.

Potter was done, and defense counsel got up to take his turn at Washburn.

"Mr. Washburn, are you sure that all three brothers were there at Nelson's that night?" said Griffin.

"Yes, I do believe that the three brothers were there, and they all left Nelson's together, leaving Love to get on his colt. I cannot recollect that Israel went away first nor in a different direction," said Washburn.

Griffin thanked him and sat back down at the defendant's table. Washburn got up and took his seat in the courtroom.

William Thompson from North Boston was called next.

"Where did you see John Love on the evening of December fifteenth, Mr. Thompson?" said Potter.

I believe that Thompson was one of the groups of people who found Love's body on that day in February.

"I saw John on his colt passing the sawmill with Nelson and Israel. They crossed the bridge going toward Israel's. One of the brothers was just ahead of them," said Thompson.

Potter asked, "And how far is Israel's from the sawmill?"

Thompson answered, "The sawmill is about three-fourths of a mile from Israel's. I can't say positively that I saw Isaac there, but Israel was ahead and crossed the bridge first before Nelson and Love."

"Thank you, Mr. Thompson," finished Potter.

Thompson left the witness stand and then, in a surprise move that caused a gasp emanating around the gallery, the district attorney called Sally Thayer, Nelson's wife to the stand. After the initial astonishment at Potter's next witness, not a sound was heard in the room but the rustling of her petticoat as Sally walked slowly and hesitantly to the front of the room, raising her right hand and swearing on the Bible that she would only tell the truth. Her husband had been charged with murder most foul, and yet she held her head high and spoke firmly and clearly.

Potter began, "Mrs. Thayer, I thank you for coming today, and I will try not to upset you with my questions. Did you know John Love?"

"Yes," she said, "I knew John Love well."

Mr. Potter asked her, "And when was the last time you saw him?"

"The last time I saw him was at our house. I do not recollect the day, but it was toward evening," she said.

"And was your brother-in-law, Isaac, there as well?" asked Mr. Potter.

"Isaac was there in the morning and went away to Obed Gwynns for a spell and then returned in the afternoon," said Sally.

"Mrs. Thayer," asked Mr. Potter, "can you tell us what transpired that afternoon and early evening on the day you last saw John Love?"

"Later that afternoon, Israel was also at the house, and Love came there soon after. Israel asked Nelson to go and help him cut up his hogs that he had butchered that morning, and Nelson told him he'd come the next morning instead. He said the pork wouldn't spoil overnight. Israel asked Love if he wanted to come to his house for the night. Love declined and said he would stay with us that night. Then Nelson concluded to go help Israel, and Isaac also consented to accompany them on Israel's request to cut up the pork. They all asked John to go with them, and he said, 'As long as everyone is going, I might as well go also,'" explained Mrs. Thayer.

"And then what happened?" asked the bard.

"Well, it was about sundown when they all left together. Of course, it took John a little longer to get going—he was having trouble getting on his colt," said Sally.

"Did any of the men take a rifle with them?" asked Mr. Potter.

"No, I did not see any of them holding a rifle or taking one with them. I have not seen John since that time either," Mrs. Thayer said.

"Thank you, Mrs. Thayer, and what if anything happened the next morning?" asked Potter.

She said, "Isaac came by the house the next morning, even before I awoke. He didn't live with us—he made his home at Samuel Washburn's."

"Approximately when was that do you think?"

"It was between daylight and sunrise when he came. He refused breakfast. I thought he said he had breakfast at Samuel's."

"And how long did your brother-in-law stay at your house that morning?" asked Potter.

"He stayed but a few minutes. Then he went on to Samuel's house," she said.

"Now, Mrs. Thayer, how far is your house from Israel's and from Washburn's?" asked Potter.

She said, "Washburn's is nearby my house. Our house is between Israel's and Washburn's along the same road."

"I beg your indulgence, counselor," spoke up Judge Walworth, "I'd like to ask the witness a few questions of my own. The answers to these questions might possibly have a bearing upon a subsequent trial. If you wish, those jurors not sworn on this trial could retire from the room."

Counsel made a waving motion with his hand, and so the unsworn jurors left the room. Mrs. Thayer adjusted her seat, and her petticoats made a hushed sound as she sat back down. She looked a little frightened that the judge would want to ask her questions himself.

"Mrs. Thayer," said the judge, "do you have any children?"

"Yes, judge, I have children. The oldest is about five years of age," she said falteringly.

"And was anyone but the children there with you that night after you saw your husband and company depart for Israel's house?" asked the judge.

"Just my children and Laura Willson, who sometimes stays with me overnight."

The judge asked, "Who is Laura Willson?"

"She is a thirteen-year-old orphan girl who used to stay with us, but now she stays at Samuel's. She sometimes comes back to stay with me," said Sally. "She surprised me by coming over to stay the night."

"Did she stay with you until morning?" asked the judge.

"Yes, she was there in the morning when Isaac came over," she said.

"And when did your husband come back home?" asked the judge.

She answered, "Nelson came back home in the morning."

The judge asked, "Is that normal for your husband to stay away all night?"

"Yes, he frequently stayed away all night, especially when he helps his brothers with their crops or livestock," Sally answered.

The judge was done with his questions and excused her from the witness stand. Sally gingerly stepped down from the witness stand, the swishing of her petticoats the only sound in the room.

The clock tower down the street chimed the hour as half past one, so the judge called for a recess of one hour to be followed by more testimonies. Two constables were sworn to take charge of the jury, and the jurors were charged to refrain from all conversation on the subject of this trial among themselves or with others and to take their refreshments together.

My companion and I took our leave of the courthouse and walked several blocks to a pub we passed on the way into town. We shook the wet snow off our coats and boots as we sat at a table. We were informed that all they had to offer in the way of victuals was some cold meat and some bread. We agreed that that would be fine, and the girl left for the kitchen to prepare our request.

There were many other people from the courthouse there who were entertaining their supper. The room was abuzz with comments, opinions, and gasps. As they all spoke in hushed tones, I could not hear their exchanges.

My friend opened the conversation by asking me if this was the first trial I had ever been a party to.

"Oh, yes," I replied with a nervous laugh. "My life has only been graced with taking care of women in childbirth or the elderly dying of consumption. My position as county coroner has not been needed very often as most deaths are of natural causes. When I was sent to examine the body in Boston, I was quite surprised. When I got there the next day, I was sickened by the extent of the wounds that were inflicted on the poor man. I have seen men who have fallen off of roofs or have had a flintlock explode in their hands, but never have I seen the effects of an axe wound to the head and neck and rifle shot to the same body.

"To think that someone had caused these wounds purposefully would be…as if to look the devil right in the eye. What could have taken a man's heart to cause him to hate so completely, so encompassing as to exert such wounds on another's person." I shook my head with utter dismay that this kind of hatred exists within a man's soul.

"It is shocking to think that this could happen in a small village like Boston," agreed Dr. Gould. "I know most of the residents of North Boston very well. Most are hardworking people and have centered their lives around God's teachings.

"I have also had some dealings with the Thayers in the past. Their respect for their women is sorely lacking. I found that out when one of them came to my office with a cut hand. And I advised him to have his wife change the bandage every day, and he was vehement that he would do it himself and muttered some insults about his wife that were rather off-putting. They are all married, and I could only hope that their wives' influence might tame their basal souls and instill in them respect at least for human life, especially as they all have children of their own," he continued.

"They all have children!" I exclaimed. "May God bless them! These men surely prove that God does not dictate the lives of everyone. Now, Emmons, you are assuming that these brothers have been proven to have done this filthy deed," I reminded him. "Does not our legal system assume that a man is innocent until it is proven that he is guilty?" Though in my mind, I believed that this trial would come to the foregone conclusion of the men's guilt.

My friend and I enjoyed a good meal of mutton and biscuits and then returned to the courthouse to witness more of the day's proceedings.

Chapter 4, Part 2
THE TRIAL

We returned to the courthouse after our repast and found that our seats up front had already been taken, so we found two seats together on the other side of the room. The room was getting uncomfortably tightly packed as witnesses and spectators alike tried to get a seat.

Pardon Pierce was the next witness called to the witness stand.

Mr. Potter got up again to volley more questions to this witness. "Mr. Pierce, please tell this jury where you reside and what you heard and saw on the fifteenth of December last."

"Well, sir," began Pierce, "I live about a mile from Israel Thayer's, nearly north. About the fifteenth of December last, I heard a report of a gun in the night at late bedtime, say nine or ten o'clock, a little east of south, very nearly in the direction of Israel Thayer's."

Mr. Potter interrupted him. "Mr. Pierce, how can you be sure that this occurred on the fifteenth of December?"

"Well," Pierce said, looking up like he was trying to extract a memory for the area of his brain, "I know it was before…the eighteenth of December. I finished clapboarding my house on Saturday the eighteenth. My wife was absent when I heard the gun report, and being outdoors, when I heard it, I recollect that the ends of my new house were clapboarded. But the sides were not. So I believe that the gun was fired the week before the Saturday that I finished."

"Thank you, please focus on the gun report you heard," Potter said.

"I thought at first that the sound came from Irish's, but I did not think at the time that it came from Thayer's. Irish lives about fifty rods from the Thayer's. On hearing the report, it first struck me that they might be shooting at candles as was sometimes the case at Nelson's. He sometimes would light a candle and then shoot it out for target practice. But the report was not in that direction but more directly from Israel's."

"Thank you, Mr. Pierce, for your intimate knowledge of the Thayers' target practice habits. No more questions," said Potter frowning.

A wave of stifled laughter could be heard throughout the room.

Another attorney for the prisoners got up to cross-examine Pierce. "Mr. Pierce, how can you tell this court from whence the report was heard, when you live nearly a mile away?"

"Sir, the direction of the report was not far from either Irish's or Israel's. I lately ranged the distance by some trees and found it to bring me somewhere between the two houses," said Pierce.

"Fine then," said the counselor, "but couldn't the report you heard have come from a musket? Perhaps someone shooting at a deer or raccoon?"

Pierce looked shocked at the question and said, "I think, sir, that I can distinguish between the reports of rifles and that of muskets. Muskets give a longer report and can be heard further. It was my first impression at the time that this was a report from a rifle. Yes, I fully believe it was a rifle."

Mr. Pierce was excused, and he left the courtroom through the back door. I don't know if he intended to leave just then, or if he noticed that his seat in the gallery had been taken by other spectators. The room was still at over full capacity with people lining the walls surrounding it.

Betsey Rector, daughter of Nicholas Rector, was called up to speak next. She walked briskly to the witness' seat and settled into the chair.

Mr. Potter began his questioning, asking her to tell the court where she lived and what she remembered about that day in December.

"I live about half a mile nearly west of Israel's with my father. I heard a report of a gun on the evening of the fifteenth of December, as I believe. It was on Wednesday, the week before Christmas, which was the second Sunday after, at ten or eleven o'clock in the evening. It appeared to be in the direction of Irish's, probably after ten o'clock," she offered.

Mr. Potter then asked her, "How far do you live from Irish's and from Israel's?"

"The distance," she said, "from our house to Irish's and to Israel's is about the same."

"What kind of night was it, or rather, what was the weather like?" Potter asked.

"It was not a light night," she said. "There was no moon shining that night, so it was cloudy. And there was a little snow on the ground. When I heard the report, I thought that maybe Irish was preparing early for the turkey shoot on Christmas Day."

Mr. Potter handed her off to the prisoner's counsel.

Counsel for the defense (I found out later that his name was Mr. Allen) got up and asked her how well she knew John Love.

"Oh, I knew him fairly well," she said with a look of a tiny bit of excitement that turned into a sorrowful look. "On the Monday previous, Mr. Love had requested me to make some clothes for him, and he said he would fetch them there the next Saturday, on which day I heard he was gone." She looked down sadly.

Mr. Allen asked, "What did you think of that?"

Betsey said, "I was disappointed that I had worked on the clothes, and he didn't seem to be there to pick them up. But then I heard (gasp!) suspicions of his murder before any of the Thayer brothers were taken up by the constable."

"Let's go back to the night you heard the report of the gun," said Allen. "Did anyone else in the household hear the report?"

"On the evening that I heard the gun fired, Mrs. Andrews came to visit us. My mother inquired why she did not bring Israel's wife with her. Mrs. Andrews and Mrs. Thayer came often to visit together. Mrs. Andrews said that it seemed that Mr. Thayer was killing hogs for the market when I asked her to come here with me, and she said that she had to stay and help him."

"So did you think that the report of the gun had something to do with the killing of the hogs?" asked Allen.

"Oh, no," she said, "you don't kill hogs with a gun. You cut their throat!"

Nervous laughter filled the room, and Betsey shrunk back as she realized that the bard knew nothing of killing hogs for the market. But then, why should he know how to kill a hog when he'd probably never done so?

"But did anyone else in the household hear the gun?" asked Allen again, although sheepishly.

"I was in the doorway at the time I heard the gun, and all the rest of the family were in bed. They might have heard it as well as I. I don't have any knowledge of that," she finished.

As the afternoon wore on, it appeared that the district attorney had every intention of asking everyone in town what they experienced that night for he next called Abigail Andrews to the witness stand.

Mr. Potter only had two questions for Mrs. Andrews. "Mrs. Andrews, were you at the Rector's home on the fifteenth of December last, and did you stop at Mrs. Thayer's house to see if she wanted to go along?"

Mrs. Andrews said, "Yes, I visited Mrs. Rector and Betsey on that day. I stopped at the Thayer's house to see if Mrs. Thayer wanted to come along. But her husband was killing hogs, so she had to stay."

"Your witness!" said Mr. Potter to Mr. Allen.

Mr. Allen got up quickly as he had just sat down from questioning Miss Rector. He fumbled around some papers as he prepared to question Mrs. Andrews.

"Mrs. Andrews," he said, "how can you recollect that it was the fifteenth of December?"

I think he was trying to confuse her on the date.

"I recollect it, young man, from the fact that I had a particular conversation with Mrs. Rector regarding a very personal subject!" she said.

Not wanting to delve into Mrs. Andrews' "personal subject" as she was an older lady and didn't seem to take kindly to interrogatories into her personal life, Mr. Allen said, "Does your husband kill hogs at this time of year as well?"

"Yes," she said, "Mr. Andrews' hogs were killed on the Saturday before this Wednesday, which was a week before Christmas."

"And how far away do you live from Israel Thayer's house?" asked Allen.

"I live about forty rods south of Israel's," she replied.

"Did you spend the night at Mrs. Rector's that night?" asked Allen.

"Certainly not!" she exclaimed. "I went home before sundown and was at home all night."

Mr. Allen had one more question for the lady. "Did you hear the report of a gun that night?"

"Well, Mr. Andrews did come to bed and asked me who could be shooting at so late an hour, but I do not recollect hearing it that night or any other night for that matter," she replied.

Mr. Allen, looking like he was thankful for the end to his questioning of Mrs. Andrews, excused her and allowed her to go back to sit with her husband.

Benjamin Sprague was the next resident of North Boston to be questioned. Dr. Gould told me during the murmurings in the gallery between witnesses that Benjamin had just turned twenty this past March and was working as a carpenter. He had just returned to North Boston after returning to his family's native city of Bennington, Vermont, to find a wife. He returned with a beautiful lady by the name of Aurillia Millington, who had just married him some weeks before.

Benjamin testified that he lived about half a mile from Israel Thayer's, nearly northeast. He heard a report of a gun on the fourth day of the week, on the fifteenth of December. He and his wife thought it was nearly eleven o'clock in the evening. The report seemed to be about Israel's house.

He testified that he was in the search party to look for Love's body, and once found, he began to reflect on the time he heard the gun. His wife first recollected it and reminded him about hearing the gun so late at night. He at first thought that maybe someone was trying to scare away an owl from a flock.

The next witness up to the stand was a complete surprise to me and to all those in attendance. I believe that a child should be spared the horrors of discussing something as heinous as murder. The next witness was a young boy of perhaps eleven or twelve years of age. He went to sit in the witness seat that seemed to swallow him up; he was so small. He stated that his name was Daniel A. Pierce, son of Pardon Pierce, and that he could read some but could not write.

The judge spoke to him next, "Now, Daniel, you understand that when you take an oath in a courtroom, you cannot lie. And you must tell all you know when asked a question on a subject. Do you understand that?"

"Yes, sir!" young Daniel said with a certain ferocity.

Everyone chuckled a little at his eagerness. He was sworn the oath, and Mr. Potter began the questions.

"Where," asked Potter, "were you living at the time back in December last, Daniel?"

Daniel began, "I lived at Israel Thayer's when he killed his hogs, to help him. Israel told me after we killed the hogs I might go home and stay with my family that night. He gave me a hog's pluck to carry to my mother."

"A hog's pluck. Now what is that, Daniel?" asked Potter.

"It's the innards. You know, the parts you can cook down for soups, like the heart, liver, and tongue. It was given to me as payment for helping out at the farm," advised Daniel.

"Well, that's mighty fine. And did you stay at Israel's house that night?" asked Potter.

"No, sir, I went home and stayed all night," said Daniel.

"Now, Daniel," asked Potter, "did you ask Israel if you could go home that night, or was it his idea?"

"Well," said Daniel, "I asked him a couple of times in the past if I could go home for the night, and he would let me go. But this time, it was his idea. He asked me if I wanted to go home that night and come back in the morning."

I wondered to myself, *Was Israel trying to get young Daniel out of the house so he and his brothers could do away with Love?* I listened intently after this to see what else the young man would say.

"Please, go on. When did you go back to Israel's?" asked Potter.

"I started back in the morning at daylight to go back to Israel's," said Daniel. "My mother and father were up when I left, and my mother made me a fine breakfast!"

Many smiles spread around the courtroom at his boyish pride!

"Then I met Isaac and Nelson going toward Nelson's house just by Sprague's house before they got to the sawmill."

"Daniel," queried Potter, "what other things would you do when you were at Israel's house on any normal day?"

"After staying the night, I would eat breakfast with them. Then Israel might ask me to go to the barn with him to feed the horses, which I did several times. Once he called me out of bed to go with him, so I could put out the hay. And he would put it in the rack."

The prisoner's counsel, Mr. Love, stood up and asked the judge what this had to do with the night of the "incident." He obviously didn't think that there must be a reason that Israel was asking Daniel to leave for the night. They could see no bearing it had upon the case unless it was to show that Israel was conscience stricken and wanted no one else around him that night.

Mr. Potter said, that with the judge's indulgence, he hoped to prove that Daniel was a necessary part of the household and that if Israel asked him to leave for the night, during the hog-killing season, it must have been a good reason.

The judge allowed the questioning of Daniel to continue. Mr. Potter thanked him and asked Daniel if Israel always brought him with him to the barn.

"Yes, sir. He always had me working on something or other," said Daniel.

"All right," rejoined Potter. "Now what did you know about Mr. Love? Mr. John Love?"

"He worked on the lake during the summer, and in the winter, he stayed with Isaac or Israel."

"And what did Mr. Love do when he stayed with Isaac or Israel?"

"Nothing much!" Daniel said with an innocence that could only be accepted from a child.

"Well," said Potter with a chuckle, "that may be, but did you see him help out with the chores on the farm?"

"Oh no! He didn't have any work clothes, and he would have only ruined the fine clothes he wore."

"So he just sat around the fire engaged in conversation?"

"Well, yes, at night after all the chores were done. But I think he rode around town visiting people most of the time," Daniel advised.

"A few days, say five or six, before we killed hogs, Mr. Love had stayed at Israel's all night. He had his colt in the barn and then he slept with me. Then later I saw his colt again in Israel's barn two or three days after we killed hogs," Daniel said. "Israel told me it was his own colt!"

"Is that right?" Potter acted surprised.

"Yes, sir! He didn't tell me if Mr. Love had given him the colt or if he had bought it from him. It was a really nice colt. But he took care of it, and it was kept there till Isaac took it away," Daniel relayed.

"Now, Daniel…this is very important. When no one had heard from Mr. Love for a time, what did Israel and his brothers have to say about his absence?" asked Potter.

"I heard the Thayers say they did not believe that Love was dead. But they also said that they were sure that he would be brought back to the county again. I don't know what they meant by that."

"And when did you hear them say that he wasn't dead when they were talking about him?" asked Potter.

"I heard this about the time that Israel came from Buffalo with pearl ashes," rejoined Daniel.

Potter shook his head a little. "Daniel, was this right after Israel killed hogs or a long time after the hogs were killed?"

"Oh! Sir, it was right after the hogs were killed," said Daniel.

"Now, Daniel, how often did Mr. Love sleep overnight at Israel's?" asked Potter.

"I only know about him staying overnight that one time. After that is when I saw the colt in Israel's barn," said Daniel.

"And had you seen Mr. Love again after you saw his colt in Israel's barn?"

"No," said Daniel, "I haven't seen him since then."

After a short pause in the conversation, Potter said, "The last time you saw Mr. Love, what was he wearing?"

"He used to wear a fur cap!" said Daniel. "He had a great coat that must have been really warm 'cause I saw him wearing it a lot in the winter. His other clothes are at my father's. They were left there after they found him…in the path under a log." Daniel looked down as he said the last few words.

"Last question, Daniel," said Potter. "How many people usually sleep at Israel's overnight, and how many beds are there in the house?"

"Well, there's Israel, his wife, and their baby who is only a couple of months old. And there's two beds—one for Israel and his wife and the baby and one for me."

"And you said that Mr. Love had shared that bed with you on the night he stayed overnight at Israel's?" questioned Potter.

"Yes, sir," said Daniel.

"Thank you, Daniel," said Potter, "you did a fine job answering my questions." He turned to the prisoner's counsel and asked them if they had any questions, and they said no.

Daniel got down from the witness stand and smiled a little, knowing that he had done his best to say the truth, as the judge told him.

My friend Emmons sat back, and a huge groan emanated from him as he switched his seating position as his left leg had fallen asleep, and the pins and needles he was experiencing were almost enough to totally paralyze it.

"Shhh!" I hushed, looking around me.

He apologized and explained his predicament in reciprocating hushed tones.

The questioning of more witnesses became more intense after Daniel's questioning. There had been other things going on behind the scenes that would shed a little more light on the prisoner's guilt that was unknown to most of us there in the room. The afternoon would see many more witnesses that would implicate the three broth-ers in more crimes than I could even keep track of, even though they were only charged with murder.

Boston resident Barney Herrington was the next to step up to the stand. Barney Herrington was not known to me. I had never met him before; I know he wasn't at the funeral at Charles Johnson's. A new prosecuting attorney got up to begin the questioning. I found out later his name was Sheldon Smith, Esq.

"Mr. Herrington," said Smith, "you have been sworn to tell this jury what occurred between you and the prisoner, Isaac Thayer, this December last. Please proceed."

Herrington began, "About the twentieth of December last, or just before Christmas, I heard Isaac say he had a note against me for wheat, which I had given John Love. We were then at Mr. Atwell's, but he did not exhibit the note. He also told Atwell that he had a note against him, which he had given to Love. I asked Isaac why he was in possession of these notes. He told me that Love had cleared out—had gone away and had given him the notes to collect for him."

"Had you heard this information before about Love?" asked Smith.

"I had heard such reports before but only from the Thayers. Then he demanded payment of the note, but he wouldn't tell me how he came by it," said Herrington incredulously.

The prisoners' counsel, Mr. Love, got up to cross-examine him.

"Mr. Herrington, did Isaac Thayer give you a reason for why Love left?" asked Love.

"I do not know as he stated any reason for Love's going away at that time," said Herrington. "I had previously heard of Love's having run away for the crime of forgery committed in Pennsylvania. I had heard it several times within a year, and I just supposed that Israel alluded to that."

"How far away from Nelson Thayer's do you live?" asked Mr. Smith.

"I live about three-quarters of a mile from Nelson's," replied Herrington.

"And how would you describe John Love?" asked Smith.

"How do you mean?" asked Herrington.

"What did he look like?" asked Smith.

"He was a short man, not five feet ten inches tall, and he weighed about 130 pounds," Herrington said.

"How old would you say he was?" Smith asked.

"I would say he was from twenty to thirty years of age," said Herrington.

"And what was his personality like?" asked Smith.

"I do not know as he was a very singular or odd man. I never saw him quarrel with anyone. He was a temperate sober man," replied Herrington.

"And do you know what his occupation was?"

"Well, for two winters, he had been in Boston trading and trafficking," replied Herrington. "In the spring, he would go up the lakes and return again in the fall. I know of no stated home or residence of his there."

"Please go on."

"He was perhaps singular in his dealings. He was a close man and made good bargains. People in town knew little of his business, except for what he did day to day," said Herrington.

Atty. Smith then asked Mr. Herrington if he had seen Love flaunting his money.

"No," said Herrington, "I never saw him have much money. I've heard of his loaning money in small sums though sometimes."

"How much is a small sum?" asked Smith.

"The largest I knew of was $60 to Nelson Thayer," said Herrington. "Generally, his loans were small and only for a month or a week."

Smith asked then, "Do you believe the body taken out of the grave back in February was that of John Love?"

"I do believe it was him. I had frequently seen him wear the trousers that were on the body when he was taken out of the grave and also his great coat. I assisted in pulling him out of the grave," replied Herrington.

With that, Mr. Smith concluded his questioning of Mr. Herrington. I thought it odd that the prisoner's counsel would ask a witness to describe the deceased while alive. I suppose he wanted to confirm that the body brought out of the shallow grave was indeed Mr. Love and not some stranger.

Wendell Morton was the next of the townspeople to testify. He said that he had heard that Love had run away. He asked Isaac where Love was. He stated that he had cleared out—gone away. Prisoner's counsel asked him if Isaac had said why he had cleared out. Mr. Morton replied that Isaac understood that Love had cleared out on account of having forged a note somewhere up the lake. Mr. Morton was then excused.

Many more witnesses got up and told of Isaac being in possession of various notes belonging to Love about Christmastime. Love had loaned money to people all over the town, and in return, they had promised him bushels of wheat at harvest time that he could sell for the money he was owed. Love would then mark the note PAID and return it to the farmer. But why was Isaac in possession of these notes? He seemingly was going about the town with many notes belonging to Love and collecting on them. This, to me, sounded rather nefarious. Why would Love leave the area and give the notes to Isaac to collect? Emmons whispered to me that he wouldn't trust Isaac to care for his dog, much less collect on someone else's debts. Was this proof that they had done away with Love and were collecting on the debts owed to him?

Sylvester Irish was next in the day's long line of witnesses. Emmons whispered to me that he was widely known and respected about town, and when Irish testified to something, it was invariably true.

Irish began his testimony in the following way: "In January, I think, I heard Isaac Thayer say that Love was gone. I knew that Isaac was collecting Love's notes, and I asked him how he had secured these notes from Love. He said he had secured them in no way. That there made me suspicious. I told him I expected that Love had notes against him for his land, and he replied that he could convince me to the contrary." Irish shook his head, insinuating that he thought Isaac was lying. "He then produced an article of a lot that was formerly

Nelson's from his pocketbook. It appeared to have been assigned to Nicholas Rector and then by him to Isaac."

"And you found that to be suspicious?" asked DA Potter.

"I did, sir!" said Irish.

"Please, go on," inquired Potter.

"At another time, Isaac came to my house after I was in bed, and he told my wife that there was a reward of $1,000 offered for information as to the whereabouts of Love. I got up out of bed and asked him where Love was. He asked my reason for the inquiry. He wasn't going to share any information and have to split the reward. I told him I just wanted to know. And again, I asked him where Love was, and he replied that he did not know." Irish continued, "I informed him that many of the townspeople thought he did know since he almost always knew if he was in town or on a trip to Buffalo. I told him that I would give him my team of oxen if he were to tell me. I even said I would include my rifle in the mix, and he answered, 'No, by God, I wouldn't even tell you for $200!'"

Many murmurs escaped the audience's lips in reaction to Isaac's alleged pledge.

"Have you ever seen Isaac with a rifle?" asked Potter.

"One morning before we were up, Isaac came in with his rifle, but I cannot say whether it was before or after the hogs were killed. And he wanted me to clean it and make it cut deeper," said Irish. "He sat it down and told me that he wanted to be there when I cut it. I told him I could not do it, but he left the rifle and went away."

"Your witness," said Potter.

Atty. Love got up and asked him, "Do you have any knowledge of a colt allegedly owned by Love?"

Irish replied, "Of course! I knew Love had a colt. I noticed that it had been at Israel's for some days. Then a few days later, I saw Isaac take him from Nelson's stable and start for Buffalo with it. He was on his way with his own horse, and I overheard Nelson tell him to take Love's colt with him as he may find 'the short fellow,' meaning Love, and if you do see him, deliver him up and let him do as he pleases with him. So Isaac led Love's colt and rode another horse. I thought this was unusual because I never knew Love to say he would trust Isaac with his property."

Mr. Love turned to the judge quickly and asked him to have that last sentence stricken from the record. He said that declarations of Love were not actual evidence but merely a declaration of the deceased, which is hearsay.

The judge agreed that Irish's last statement was only an opinion and, as such, should not be received into evidence. He requested of the court reporter that Irish's last sentence be stricken from the record.

Both sides seemed to be satisfied with Irish's statements, and he was excused from the witness stand.

Mrs. Melinda Washburn was next on the stand. I had heard that Mrs. Washburn was nobody's fool and that she spoke her mind when asked. I anticipated a rousing exchange between her and the bards on this subject.

The court clerk had her put her hand on the Bible and swear to tell the truth and then invited her to be seated.

Potter began, "Mrs. Washburn, please tell us what you remember about the events of December last regarding the disappearance of John Love?"

"Well," she said, "when Isaac was under arrest after they found Love's body, I asked him why he did not tell where Love was, and he hemmed and hawed and replied to me that Love was so damned contrary that he could get nothing out of him. He looked scared and mad all at once, and if you ask me, I think he was getting ready to soil his britches!"

A muffled titter of laughter swept through the courtroom at this unrequested opinion, and the judge was forced to slam his gavel a mite to restore order in the room.

"If you please, Mrs. Washburn, please stick to the facts at hand without adding your own interpretations of the prisoner at the time," said Potter, hiding his slight smile that he was fervently trying to squash beneath his hand. "Please tell us what transpired on December the seventeenth."

"Fine then," huffed Mrs. Washburn, acting indignant, "I believe it was December seventeenth when Isaac stayed at my house a part of the night. His father tended the sawmill and often all night. We live within calling distance of the sawmill. And his father bellowed for him about twelve o'clock or after, and Isaac got up and left. He did not return that night. This was the night after Israel's hogs were killed."

"And this was unusual behavior from Isaac?" asked Potter.

"It most certainly was!" exclaimed Mrs. Washburn. "He then returned the following morning about sunrise, telling me that he had gone to Nelson's house for breakfast. But his wife wasn't up yet, so he came to my house to eat. The idea! I told him I wasn't running a rooming house! I was up and cooking anyway, so I gave him a plate."

Mr. Potter asked, "Do you remember seeing Mr. Love around this time?"

"I think I saw him two days before that, riding toward Nelson's," she said.

"And can you say whether or not you might have heard a gunshot in the neighborhood on the last day you saw Love?" asked Potter.

"I did not," said Mrs. Washburn. "But a few nights before or after that, I did hear around ten shots toward Nelson's, and if I *had* heard a shot that night, I should not have thought it strange."

"Thank you, Mrs. Washburn," Potter said. "You may step down."

Melinda shot the judge a sideways smile, gathered up her skirts, stepped off the witness stand, and returned to her seat. Her husband, looking rather sheepish, grabbed her arm and ushered her out of the courtroom, and I never saw them again that day.

"The prosecution calls Mr. Benjamin Fowler to the stand," announced Mr. Potter.

I did not know of Mr. Fowler, and I turned to my friend and asked him if he was a resident of Boston. Emmons told me he did not think so.

"Please state your name and your town of residence for the judge," the bailiff instructed.

"If you please, judge, my name is Benjamin Fowler, and I reside in this village of Buffalo," he replied.

District Attorney Potter asked Mr. Fowler how he came to have an association with one of the prisoners.

"Well, sir," he began after clearing his throat several times, "on the twenty-third or twenty-fourth of December last, I purchased a colt from Isaac Thayer here in this village. It was a light-yellow, three-year-old colt, and I paid $40 for him. He mentioned that he was leaving the next day, on Christmas, to attend a shooting match in his hometown of Boston, and he needed to sell him before that. He was leading the colt and rode a bay mare. He said if he didn't sell the colt to me, he would take it to Batavia to sell it there. It was a fine, well-kept colt, and even though the price was high, I thought he would prove to be worth the cost."

"Thank you, Mr. Fowler, you may return to your seat," said Potter.

Mr. Fowler stepped down and went all the way to the court-house door and made his way out of it; his duty done.

I started thinking that I could see where this was going now. It was common knowledge that Love owned a light-colored, three-year-old colt; Reuben Irish had attested to that. If Isaac had sold Love's colt to Mr. Fowler the day before Christmas, Love must have been dead at that time. I fear these boys were probably indeed guilty of this crime from the evidence I had heard so far.

Judah Simons was the next Bostonian to be questioned. It went very quickly and proceeded thusly:

Mr. Potter had him sworn in by the clerk. "Repeat after me, Mr. Simons."

"I swear by Almighty God," began the clerk.

"I swear by Almighty God," said Judah.

"That I will speak the truth…"

"That I will speak the truth…"

"The whole truth…"

"The whole truth…"

"And nothing but the truth…"

"And nothing but the truth…"

"So help me God."

"So help me God."

Judah sat down, and Mr. Potter asked him what his experience was with Israel Thayer about December 20 last.

"On the twentieth of December, Israel met me on the Eighteen Mile Creek, about one mile from Nelson's," began Judah. "He was on Love's colt—a yellowish colt. He offered to sell it to me. I asked him why he was selling Love's colt. He stated that he had not bought the colt but was authorized to sell it by Isaac, who, he said, had all Love's business to transact. I was skeptical, to say the least."

"So you know the Thayer brothers well?" asked Potter.

"Yes"—Judah nodded—"I know them all too well to believe that he had permission to sell the colt."

"Did you buy the colt from Israel?"

"No!" he exclaimed. "I'd sooner buy land from a pig!"

Everyone chuckled a little at that, and Potter excused him from the witness' chair.

"The state would like to recall Sally Thayer to the witness stand if it pleases the court," said Potter.

A low murmur spread among the people in the gallery. Everyone was wondering why the district attorney would put her through questioning again. It seemed rather harsh to me to put her in front of all her neighbors again when she so obviously suffered a great deal already due to this situation. Even so, Judge Walworth waved his approval.

She got up as requested and once again mounted the witness' chair. She looked pale and shaken.

"Mrs. Thayer, I am sorry to put you through more questioning, but can you please tell the people here what went on in your household the day after Israel's hogs were killed?" he spoke in a soft, nonthreatening way.

Sally's voice was weak as she started. "Isaac came to our house in the fore part of the evening. Their father was there also and asked Isaac and Nelson if they would go to the sawmill with him and help him with a large log. They declined to do it then, and they told their father that they would get up before the sun rose the next day to help him."

"Was that normally done? To get up before the sun and start the sawmill?" asked Potter.

"Well…no…it would be too dark to see, I would think," she posited.

"And did your husband and his brother go to the sawmill the next morning?" asked Mr. Potter.

"Well," she began, "when I awoke, their father was sleeping on the floor, and Nelson and his brother were not there. They came in just at daylight, and I did not think that the sawmill had been running that night. I don't know how they would have gotten to the sawmill…we don't have any lanterns that bright."

"So you were rather confused about what happened that night and into the morning?" asked Potter.

"Well, yes," responded Sally.

"Thank you, Mrs. Thayer. Your witness, Mr. Love," said Potter.

"The defense has no questions of this witness, Your Honor," said Mr. Love.

Sally took a deep breath before she stepped away from the chair, and she was clearly relieved that it was over.

William Thompson was questioned next, and he testified that he had tended the sawmill on the fifteenth but not on the seventeenth of December. He had left some logs there to be cut on the fifteenth but did not recollect of any large ones. Mr. Potter asked him if he thought the senior Thayer would be able to tend the sawmill on his own. Thompson said that the elder Thayer was upward of fifty years old and was not a rugged man. He then stated that he had previous recollections that the father was not in the habit of sawing unless someone was with him. He was excused from the witness stand, and he sat back down with his wife, who had accompanied him to the courthouse. They then got up together and left the courtroom. A short recess was called to allow people to stretch their legs for five minutes.

When everyone had stretched and settled down again, Mr. E. Walden, Esq. was called to the stand. He was the judge who first saw the brothers after they'd been taken up from the village of Boston to fulfill the warrant against them. The line of questioning soon was to be changing direction.

"Mr. Walden, you met with the prisoners after they were arrested, is that right?" asked Potter.

"Yes, Isaac was first brought to me on a habeas corpus soon after he was arrested and brought to the jail here in the village of Buffalo. I was to fix a time for him and his brothers to produce Mr. Love or provide proof of his being alive to satisfy me. This was on a Wednesday, and the time for them to provide proof of life was affixed to the following Saturday. Constable Torrey was assigned to go find Love as I told Isaac that someone with authority must be the one to produce him to the court. Isaac said he would need no more time than that," said Walden.

"Did he have a reason for Love's disappearance?" asked Potter.

"Yes, he said he was in Canada along the river between the Bertie Ferry and Queenston, but he could not tell me the exact place," replied Walden.

"And what happened then?" asked Potter.

"Love's body was found before the Saturday deadline," answered Walden.

"Thank you, Mr. Walden, you may step down," said Potter.

What transpired next was more evidence of the brothers' erring ways and trickery that did not bode well for their innocence. The subject matter involved the many notes that Love held against various residents of the town, including the Thayers themselves.

Judge Rector from Boston was requested to sit in the witness chair next. What he confessed was troubling to me. Rector got up from his seat in the gallery and made his way up to the witness stand and was sworn.

Mr. Potter began the questioning, "What was your experience with Isaac Thayer on the seventeenth of December last?"

"Isaac was before me on the seventeenth of December to answer for Love in a suit where he was the plaintiff. He told me that Love had requested that he appear and answer for him as he was on his way to the eastern side of 18 Mile Creek, so he said. He also called on me to get Love's money in the case against Mr. Smith," explained Rector.

"Has that ever happened before regarding Love's notes against other Boston residents?" asked Potter.

"No, sir!" replied Rector. "It was highly irregular that anyone would send a representative to answer a suit in the stead of someone else."

"And were you in possession of the note that the suit was based on?" asked Potter.

"Yes, it was in my possession."

"Were you in possession of any other notes that Love had against his debtors?" asked Potter.

"I am in possession of many of Love's notes," replied Rector. "I have a demand against Isaac, amounting to $275 for which he had confessed judgments on oath, and the executions were issued."

Potter looked thoughtful and was silent for a moment before he asked the next question. "On what date were the judgments entered and the executions issued?"

"That was on the fourth of December last, and I personally gave the executions to Love," said Rector. "I haven't seen them since. I've been in possession of judgments against Israel also. I had other demands of Love's—two notes against Mr. Hilliker, about $5 to $25."

"And what about the execution against Israel?" asked Potter.

"I issued an execution against Israel for Love for $9, which was paid up to the final dollar. I had sent Constable Jones to call on Israel for it, but that day, Isaac said he had Love's power of attorney to settle it. And he had directed Jones to endorse it as satisfied," replied Rector. "It was very irregular."

"Did you know of any judgments against the elder brother, Nelson?" asked Potter.

"Love had told me sometime earlier in the presence of Isaac that he had executions against Nelson on which he wanted to sell. Love wanted Isaac to bid in the property to avoid some subsequent executions against him," replied Rector. "He wanted Isaac to bid on the judgment, so the property would be levied on as Isaac's by these executions issued by me. He did this because Love wanted to give

Nelson more time, but if the executions ran out that were levied, those other executions would attach to Nelson's property. Love was living with Nelson and didn't want to bite the hand that fed him, so to speak, by taking his property away from him at that time. I thought that was mighty big of Love to worry about Nelson's state of solvency when in the past, Love had been rather, well, extremely shrewd in his business dealings."

I started to see a sheer audacity, and I dare say, the profound foresight these brothers seemed to engender with the dealings of their debts with Love—much more maturity and cunning than I gave them credit for. This showed that if they had done away with Love, they weren't only guilty of murder but also stealing his investments.

The district attorney then produced a paper purported to be a power of attorney given to Isaac by Love, empowering him to collect, receive, settle, and compound all demands due to Love in Erie County and to defend all suits against him, bearing the date of the eighth day of January 1825. He asked Judge Rector to inspect the paper and render an opinion on its authenticity.

"Well," said Rector, "the signature is not Love's handwriting. Look here—the name isn't even spelled right. The *O* in John is omitted. This is not the first time I've seen this. The first time, the name of Nelson was not on it as a witness. At first, Isaac tried to demand Mr. Hilacher's note by verbal authority of Love."

Potter asked, "And when did this happen?"

"This was about the last of December," replied Rector. "I told him to procure a power of attorney from Love, and I refused to deliver the note or pay over money until he did."

"That was quite prescient of you, judge, may I say," said Potter. "Did he ever come up with a power?"

"Yes, he called in January for the note, or the money on it, and produced this power, but it wasn't witnessed," started Rector. "I refused to pay on it until it was witnessed. Then Isaac told me that Mr. Austin told him it was sufficient without being witnessed. I told him I didn't care what Mr. Austin had told him. In my office, a power of attorney has to be witnessed."

"And did he bring it back later with a witness?" asked Potter.

"The next time he produced it was about the twentieth of January. Nelson's name was then on it, as it now appears. I still refused to pay the money until it was also acknowledged. He was not happy. But I told him that he obviously did not know the law, and a power not only needs to be witnessed, it also needs to be acknowledged by someone with the authority to guarantee the witness's signature," Rector said with pride. "He then said he was informed that it was not necessary and mentioned something about obliging me to pay."

"What did you think of that statement?" said Potter.

"I thought it was offensive and ill-advised by 'whomever' told him that an acknowledgment was not necessary," said Rector.

"Thank you, Judge Rector," Potter concluded. "Your witness," he said to the prisoner's counsel.

Atty. Griffin got up and approached Rector and asked him how it was that he knew Love's handwriting.

Rector began with fortitude, "I am considerably acquainted with Love's handwriting, sir, but I am not much skilled in detecting forged hands. Love's writing is rather heavy—an old-fashioned hand."

Five papers were produced purporting to be Love's handwriting. Griffin showed them to Judge Rector and was asked to offer an opinion on their authenticity. He thought that two of the papers were of Love's hand, one was not his and was doubtful as to the genuineness of the others. Atty. Griffin then stated that one of the papers attested to as Love's by the judge was just then written by a member of his team. A murmur rose from the gallery, knowing that prisoner's counsel had played a trick on the judge in an effort to disqualify his opinion. Griffin excused the judge and released him to his former seat in the gallery.

I thought that was a cheap parlor trick they had committed on the judge.

Atty. S. G. Austin, the man who had allegedly told Isaac that a power need not be witnessed, was called next to testify.

Potter began his questioning, "Mr. Austin, did you draw up this power of attorney for the Thayers?"

"Yes," he agreed. "Isaac called on me to draw this power, and it is my writing. I presume it bears the date of the day it was written."

"Yes, go on," said Potter.

"They stated to me that they wanted a general power to transact all Love's business," he said.

"Was Mr. Love with them?" asked Potter.

"No, they told me that Love was in some difficulty and was apprehensive of being arrested and was secreted not far off and had sent them to obtain the power for him, which would be taken to him for his signature. I told them it was unnecessary for Love to come see me," said Austin.

"And why was that, sir?" asked Potter.

"I am also familiar with Love's hand," said Austin.

Mr. Potter then asked, "Did you advise Isaac that there was no need to have the power witnessed?"

"Yes, I did," said Austin.

"For what reason?" asked Potter.

"I advised him not to have a witness as lawsuits might follow and to obtain that witness in every case in which they used the power might be difficult," he said.

I thought to myself, *I may not be a lawyer. I'm just an average citizen, but that seemed to me to be a pretty unconvincing excuse for not getting a witness to a power of attorney.*

Austin continued, "If not witnessed, Love could prove the power himself."

"Assuming he was alive and still in the area," Potter said rather sarcastically.

"Yes, sir," Austin said, holding his head down sheepishly.

"When did this all occur?" asked Potter.

"This, I think, was in the evening of the eighth, and they represented they could obtain his signature the next day," Austin explained.

"Are you familiar with Love's handwriting?" asked Potter, trying to move the questioning in another direction.

Austin began, "I have seen him write twice, I think, and have his signatures in my office, which I have lately examined in anticipation of coming here today."

Potter showed him the power of attorney entered into evidence just prior to his questioning. "What say you on the authenticity of this example of Love's signature, Mr. Austin?"

The bard on the stand pulled his spectacles out of the breast pocket of his vest and placed them on his rather large nose in order to inspect the document offered for his opinion. He squinted through the lenses for a moment, took the glasses off his nose, and placed them back into his pocket.

He coughed a little and spoke haltingly, "Um, the signature to this power does not resemble the signatures I have filed in my office. I should think it not his." He coughed again and stayed silent.

After handing Mr. Austin to Mr. Griffin for the defense, Austin was asked his opinion on several other documents purported to have Love's signatures on them. He said he couldn't decide clearly whether the writing was Love's or not.

To further drive home the point that the power did not seem to be signed by Love, Atty. Amos Smith from the hamlet of Patchin, which lies directly between Boston and North Boston, was called to the stand next. The young attorney lowered himself slowly into the witness seat and straightened his waistcoat, taking extra care to smooth the silk edges so they wouldn't curl.

He told those in the room that Love had left a note with him for collection against Caleb Pierce. Isaac had presented the power to him and demanded the money to be collected presently. He said he refused to pay Isaac the money he had collected from Caleb because he thought the power was incomplete.

Potter asked him, "How so?"

He said that the power had not been witnessed. He said that Isaac went away annoyed and returned later that day with Nelson's name and signature on it as a witness.

Potter asked him, "Did you pay the money to Isaac that you collected from Caleb at that time?"

"No!" he said. "I refused the document because I felt it was a forgery. It couldn't be Love's signature on it as the witness is supposed to *witness* Love signing it. That couldn't be what happened. By the way, John Love had good penmanship. He was in my office often, writing various documents in front of me. In fact, the first time the power was presented to me, it looked to me that the signature was in Nelson's writing. Nelson sometimes writes well, sometimes not. The letters in Nelson's signature are longer than Love's generally and more erect."

"Did Isaac then actually file a complaint against you for not paying on Caleb Pierce's note?" Potter asked, incredulous.

"To my surprise, yes!" answered Mr. Smith. "I was called to a court led by Atty. Swain in Boston. Isaac charged me with falsely denying the power and judgment was rendered against me. Therefore, I had to pay Isaac the money I collected from Caleb. While at court, I overheard either Isaac or Nelson say he had seen Love within the last few days."

"And when did this all happen?" asked Potter.

"I was at Swain's court on the fifteenth of February."

"On what date did you first see this power of attorney?" asked Potter.

"I first saw it on Monday, the tenth of January. I got the idea that Isaac was trying to hide something. So I told Isaac that if Love was afraid of being arrested, he might call on me in the night, and I would pay him rather than use power to collect the money. I thought he must have been in the neighborhood as the power was dated on the eighth, and this was only on the tenth. Then Isaac said something I thought quite curious at the time," said Smith.

"And what was that?" asked Potter.

"He said, 'My god, Love could not visit with you. He is a damned sight farther off than people here have any idea of.'"

Everyone in the room gasped at that revelation, and Potter excused Mr. Smith from the witness stand. My companion and I exchanged troubled glances at each other as Mr. Smith revealed that last statement. Had Isaac almost admitted that he knew that in no way John Love could have visited Smith from beyond the grave?

Benjamin Dole was called next to the front of the courtroom. I took a long deep breath as I realized that on this day, I had listened to the stories of practically every citizen of the little village of Boston with regard to John Love—a man I never met, yet I felt like I had known him all my life. So many people knew him and described him and his actions in such a way that I felt like I experienced all he had experienced in the latter months of the year 1824.

Twenty-year-old Ben Dole, only one year older than Isaac Thayer, testified that he had seen Isaac the Saturday after Love was reported to be missing. He seemed to have had a considerable amount of money rolled up in his pocket. He could not estimate the value, only that it looked to be fifteen or twenty-some odd bills.

"Did that seem odd to you at the time, Mr. Dole?" asked Potter.

"Isaac never had any money in his pocket. When I saw the roll of bills," said Ben, "I saw that he had them all in Love's pocketbook."

"How did you know it was Love's pocketbook?"

"I frequently saw him with it," said Ben.

"Isaac had been owing me for a year before this," Ben continued, "and he was always complaining that he could not get any extra money to pay me. He owed me about $20. I had to get a judgment against him to make him pay."

"At this time in December last, did he finally pay off the judgment?" asked Potter.

"Yes, I finally collected it from him," said Ben. "I also had a judgment against Israel Jr. for $5 or $6, which he was supposed to pay me in December, but I waited until January. He paid me then."

Ben was thanked and excused from the stand.

The next witness to testify proved to be very informative. Constable Erastus Torrey was asked next to be questioned. I found out later that the Torrey family was one of the first settlers in the village of Boston. In point of fact, the village now known as Boston was once called "Torrey's Corners." It was a very large family, and they made their homes south of the area where the alleged murder took place in the hamlet of North Boston. Needless to say, Constable Torrey's testimony was considered reliable and true to the facts.

"Good afternoon, Constable Torrey," began Potter, "please describe, if you could, the person of John Love as you knew him."

Torrey, sitting tall and stiff in the witness chair, began in a booming voice, "Love was a very shrewd man. He made a lot of money working on the Great Lakes in the summer. Then when he started renting from the Thayers, when people in the neighborhood were needing a little money to get them through a rough spot, he would lend it to them and hold a promissory note against them."

"And what would he demand as payment?" asked Potter.

"Sometimes he would want money, sometimes he would demand bushels of grain or even a piece of land, depending on the dollar amount of the loan and what he determined that the person was most likely to be flush with when it came time to pay up," said Torrey.

"In your opinion, Constable Torrey, were the people in town likely to borrow a great deal of money from Love? Why would they attach a piece of land to the judgment when land was hard to come by in and of itself?" asked Potter.

"The people in our town," started the constable, "are very poor. For anyone to have an extra dollar or two just doesn't happen. These people are always struggling to live day to day. Robbing Peter to pay Paul was a daily reality. So it was not unusual for a family to need to lay in food to eat that very day, so they would go to Love and request a loan to get by until they could take their crops into Buffalo, and then they could pay him back. That's why he might demand a certain percentage of their crops in payment for the loan."

"All right, that being said," asked Potter, "you must have been called upon to collect on these debts for Love."

"That is very true. I had an execution for Ben Dole against Isaac after he was arrested and put in jail. His attorney, Mr. T. C. Love, sent me the money for the execution. Isaac must have had the money on him when he was arrested. So I gave it to Ben and satisfied the judgment," said Torrey.

"Thank you. Now let's go to the power of attorney held by Isaac for John Love," began Potter. "You saw it, and in your opinion, was it a lawful power?"

"I did see it and examined the signature, and I believe it *not* to be Love's writing. As I said earlier, I was very familiar with Love's writing due to the several judgments he held against townspeople."

"Now if you could please regale the gathering here with a conversation you had with Isaac this past January," said Potter.

"In the early part of January last, I told Isaac at my house that Love's judgments against him needed to be paid back, even though he held the power and Love was away. He replied to me, 'Give yourself no uneasiness. I have the payments in my pocket right now.'

"I took him aside and approached a subject that was bothering me, although I was uncertain what I might have to do, depending on his answers," said Torrey.

"And what was that?" asked Potter.

"I told him that people supposed that he had murdered Love, (a gasp was heard in the room) and that he had better find Love and produce him if he could," Torrey explained.

"And what was his reaction?" asked Potter.

"He got very angry and said he could produce him with no hesitation, but he would be damned if he would!" finished Torrey.

Thank you, sir, for your testimony," said Potter, "you may step down."

My companion and I were thoroughly exhausted by this point in the trial. Our minds were reeling with all the testimony and how damning it seems to be for the Thayers. They were already maligned as poor, uneducated lugs who spent all their free time drinking and being lazy. So if the accounts of the area merchants and neighbors alike are to be believed, the young men had actually conceived and committed a profoundly heinous crime and uncharacteristically showed remarkable insight and inventiveness in their cover-up of Love's disappearance. It was enough to make one dizzy at the prospect.

It was well past the supper hour, but there were more witnesses to speak, and Judge Walworth excused the room for a short time. I was never more thankful for a handle of dried meat and a crust of bread my wife had the forethought to pack for me.

After a short quarter of an hour, the judge recalled everyone to their seats, and the testimonies continued. I feared that I may not be able to stay awake and focus on the remaining witness' testimonies, but I made up my mind to stay as sharp as I could manage.

James Ives was called up, and he testified that about the tenth of January, he noticed that Isaac had considerable money on his person, and he paid him two executions he had against Israel and Nelson, in all, about $17. Then Isaac told him that he had money left—enough to pay all the debts anyone could bring against him or his brothers. From the murmurings in the room, it seemed that people knew that Isaac being flush with money was just as unlikely as the moon stepping down from the heavens and landing in Buffalo harbor. Mr. Ives was excused, and he left the courtroom through the front door behind us.

Orin Trent, another Boston constable, testified next that he was trying to collect on an execution dated the eighth of November in favor of James Ives against Israel in the amount of $10. Israel was nowhere to be found. He made search for him, but he expected that he kept out of his way. Then he finally saw him in January after he had returned the execution to Ives. Israel told him that he had visited with Ives and paid him the execution. Then he started bragging that even after paying Ives off, he had enough money left over to take care of any other executions against him and his brothers.

This being corroborating testimony that the Thayers were bragging about having money, the people in the room started murmuring again, and the murmur rose to a din until the judge slammed down his gavel and demanded order in the court.

Then the questioning turned to Mr. John Twining, who told a story of the last time he saw Love.

"I saw him last on the fourteenth of December," he began, "he came to me in my lot, which is about eighty rods from Nelson's. He asked me if I was going to Buffalo anytime soon. I told him that I planned on making a trip the very next day, and I asked him why he was asking."

"And what was his reason?" asked Potter.

"He said that his former employer, Joseph Bennett, owed him his last day's pay and asked me if I would collect it from him in Buffalo if he gave me an execution against him. I said I would, and we went to Atty. Austin's to draw up the paperwork."

"Then what happened with the execution the next day?" asked Potter.

"I went to Buffalo and, after my business was done, went to the harbor to look for Bennett. I found him, but he told me that he had sent his father, Samuel, to Boston that very day to pay Love what he owed him. He described his father to me, so I might know him if I saw him on the road," said Twining.

"Well, that certainly was helpful of him," said Potter.

"Oh, yes, it was positively providential," said Twining laughing, "because I did see him on the road back to Boston. He was coming out as I was traveling in. He was exactly as young Bennett had described, right down to the kind of buckboard he was using."

"And what was the conversation you had with the elder Bennett?" asked Potter.

"Well, he asked me if I knew where Love was," said Twining. "I told him that I did not, but perhaps he was at Nelson's. He told me he looked for him there and did not find him. We then talked about the money his son, Joseph, owed Love, and since I held the execution given to me by Atty. Austin, he gave me the money to give to Love."

"Then did you see Love upon your return to Boston and give him the money Bennett owed him?" asked Potter.

"No," said Twining, "it was late when I got back so I waited until the next day. Then I went up to Nelson's, and that was when Isaac showed me the power of attorney paper that he had that entitled him to collect on any of Love's debts. I asked him where Love was that he would have him to collect his debts, and he just said he was 'away,' so I gave the money to him."

A very audible "Ah!" arose from those seated as they were able to connect the dots between the time that Twining said he gave Isaac the money and when Isaac went around town, paying off the debts he and his brothers owed. Again, the murmurs became too loud, and the judge had to use his gavel to ask for quiet in the room.

"Thank you, Mr. Twining, you may step down," spoke Potter loudly so as to be heard above the clamor.

It was at that time that Judge Walworth adjourned the court with an admonition that the trial would resume the next day at 8:00 a.m. Tongues and attention spans were tired, and the fires in the two fireplaces that heated the room were dying. The two court constables were sworn to attend the jury and keep them together until 8:00 a.m.

the next morning. The jurors were charged to avoid all conversation on the subject of the cause before them until the next morning. The whole experience was so enthralling, so mind consuming, that Dr. Gould and I decided to stay on to view the second day of testimony, both for our enlightenment and for the enlightenment of our friends and neighbors when we went back home and retold the testimony we witnessed and the damning evidence that was to prove the Thayers brothers' guilt.

*****

At half past 8:00 a.m. on the twenty-second day of April 1825, the court resumed its austere attempt to prove or disprove the Thayers brothers' guilt of the crime of murder against one John Love—war hero, philanthropist, salesman, and sailor. My companion and I had arisen early in order to arrive at the courthouse to command the same seats we had the day before. I felt a kind of ashamed anticipation of what new facts might appear today, whether it would be boring or lurid. The attorneys on both sides had planned their approach to either defense or prosecution, and it was time they plied their trade.

Reuben Irish was asked to sit on the witness stand once more.

"Mr. Irish, be aware that you are still under oath," warned Judge Walworth.

"Yes, sir" was Irish's reply.

"Mr. Irish," began the district attorney. "Please refresh our collective memories of your testimony yesterday forenoon."

"Well, sir, I was saying that on the night of December 15, I went to Washburn's coalpit. I was not there any other night that week. As I traveled to Washburn's, I heard gunfire."

"Which direction were you traveling, Mr. Irish?" asked Potter.

"I was traveling eastwardly to the coalpit. Israel's house was then east or northeast of me. The coalpit was, say, ten or twelve rods from Israel's home," said Irish.

"And from which direction did you hear the gunfire?"

"The gun's report was behind me. I do not know what time of night it was."

The defense attorney then cross-examined Irish.

"Mr. Irish, you say you do not know what time of night it was that you traveled to Washburn's coalpit? Was it right after sunset? Was it closer to midnight? Surely you could narrow the possibilities a little," said Atty. Griffin.

Irish replied rather sheepishly, "Well, now that I think about it, I did have a conversation with Washburn's apprentice, Mr. Congleton, about two weeks after that night and tried to figure out which part of the night it was. We figured that I went out to the coalpit the first time a little after dark. I then went up to Washburn's house, where his wife was still up. I left again to check on the coalpit, and that was when I heard the report when I was about halfway there. It was still the fore part of the night, but I cannot recollect the exact time."

Griffin thanked Irish for his testimony and told him to step down from the witness chair.

Next up was Frederick Jones. He had previously testified that he was part of the group that found Love's body back in February. Jones was a wiry little man who spoke so quickly that you had to strain to hear everything he said. The DA asked him what his relationship was with the Thayers before the incident.

"Just about the same 'lationship as mos' people," he said. "They was just a bunch of drunkards who treated everyone, includin' their animals, like they was dirt."

Continuing, Potter asked him about a pocketbook he found at Nelson's.

"After the boys was arrested, I did find a pocketbook at Nelson's the night after we found Love's body in a chest in his bedroom, containing over $300 of Love's demands."

I did a double take and looked at my friend Emmons as an audible gasp escaped from those in attendance at this testimony of the exorbitant amount of money that Love had lent to people.

Potter spoke quickly, "So you took it upon yourself to go through Nelson's house without his permission?"

"We was asked by the authorities to see if we could find any evidence that would show that the boys made plans to murder Love."

"Well, maybe Love had lost his pocketbook, and Nelson put it in safekeeping to return to him when it was convenient," commented Potter.

"I don't believe that. When we was looking for Love's body, he never mentioned that he had found it and wanted to return it," corrected Jones.

A slow hum went around the room in agreement with Jones's testimony.

"Did you ever hear any of the brothers talking about Love, perhaps in private?"

"I overheerd Nelson telling Isaac about Love goin' away—it was soon after Love went missin'," said Jones. "He said that Love had cleared out after a stranger had come lookin' for him. Isaac saw me standin' there and whispered to Nelson to hush. I also heerd them saying something about Love committin' a forgery, and he was afraid the stranger was come to git' 'im. So he cleared out."

"Did you know Love well?" asked the DA.

The answer was "I did know him well…he was a close man. Kept to himself mostly. Real careful of his interests."

"Thank you, Mr. Jones. Mr. Love, your witness."

"The defense has no questions, Your Honor."

Two more witnesses were called to the stand, but their testimony only involved demands and executions that Love held and when they should be paid. I could not fathom why the prosecutor would bring these people to testify when it seemed not to contain anything that would lead one to believe that Love had been murdered by the Thayers. My eyes were getting bleary and needed some rubbing to wake them up, and I fear I let out a great yawn, which I could not suppress. I got looks of warning from the prosecutor's table, and I felt myself shrinking down in my seat.

I had to abandon all hope of the preceding testimonies being sufficient proof that the Thayers committed the crime or not as several more witnesses were to testify. Sylvester Irish was brought back to the witness stand to continue answering the queries of the attorneys tasked with bringing to light every crumb of evidence that could be had.

"The gun used for the shooting of John Love was found in your home, Mr. Irish," commented Mr. Potter. "How do you explain that?"

"The gun truly belongs to Isaac," Irish explained quickly. "He brought Israel's wife to visit us, and he had to run back home to gather some things she forgot. He had his gun with him then, and he stood it up next to the fireplace while he ran home. I laid down on the floor, but I do not recollect whether I took off my boots and stockings. It was late in the evening. I have no recollection when the rifle was taken away from my house—it might have been that night, or it may have been on the night they were killing hogs."

"Thank you, Mr. Irish."

"No questions, Your Honor."

Then came the testimony of Charles Howard. He had seen all four Thayers on Christmas at Arnold's at the shooting match that he sponsored. The shooting match was a tradition on Christmas for the townspeople—a sixpence a shot toward a group of turkeys that had been corralled within fencing. Isaac had several bank bills which, to us, were extremely irregular. They came quite early and shot a few times first, then Israel and Nelson told Isaac to give him a $3 bill and let him keep his own account until they had shot out the money. This was so out of character for that family; it raised more than just the eyebrows of the people in the room. Then Isaac gave him a $2 bill and said he had enough money and that he was not afraid of mere sixpences. Everyone in the room gasped at such flagrant disregard for the value of the money they were using to shoot turkeys with, which begs the question, how did they get so flush with paper money?

Atty. Daniel Swain of Boston then testified to his examination of Isaac Thayer after he had been arrested on the nineteenth of February last.

"Mr. Swain, can you please tell us what transpired on that day when you questioned Isaac Thayer?" asked Potter.

"The prisoner was charged with murdering John Love and plead 'not guilty,'" he said." Then he told me the last time he saw Love was in Boston, near the lower schoolhouse. His brother Nelson was also with him. He said that Love talked candidly about his forging and other embarrassments for which he expected to be pursued. So in anticipation of his leaving town, Love gave over all his obligations to Isaac to collect for him in his absence and had Nelson witness the contract. Love then departed in haste sometime in December last at sunrise. He did not remember the exact date. He told me that he had seen Love twice since then. The first time was several weeks later, and the second time was four or five weeks past and not less than four weeks past. Both times he saw him in a field with no one else around and no explanation of what he was doing in the field or whose field it was. He said he had not seen Love in any house or with anybody either time."

"Thank you, Mr. Swain, for your testimony."

There were several other witnesses who testified to seeing Isaac flaunting the fact that he had paper money in his possession, the schedule of the demands that were discovered in Love's pocketbook, the fact that one of the brothers had sold Love's colt and had the money on him, and the residents of the town's recognition of Love's clothes and great coat that were on the body that was found buried behind Isaac's home. The rapidity with which the witnesses testified and were excused caused my head to swim with all the information. I hoped that those in charge of this display could keep everyone's story straight.

Mr. Potter then stood behind the prosecutor's table and advised the judge that the prosecution rested.

After noting in his record that the prosecution rested its case, the judge took a recess at half past one o'clock for one hour in the same form as the day before. I for one was exceedingly grateful.

The hour flew by like the flight of a frightened dove, and the afternoon was to consist of the defendant's case as prepared by the defense counsel's table.

Mr. Thomas Love, no relation to the decedent, began his discourse thusly:

"Gentlemen of the jury, the embarrassments under which I rise to address you, on the subject of this defense, is beyond the power of language to express. On the one hand is a rigorous prosecution for the most *damning* of all offenses, conducted by an able, industrious, and persevering prosecuting attorney, assisted by two associate counsel of distinguished ability and great professional skill. And on the other hand, the lives of two fellow human beings, in some measure, committed to my care and staked upon the result of the issue I am called upon to defend.

"May I not with propriety express myself in the language of inspiration and ask, 'Who is sufficient for these things?'

"I have not infrequently addressed a jury of my country from this place on subjects involving the pecuniary interest, character, and in some instances, the personal liberty of an anxious and confiding client, but it is the first time it has ever occurred in the course of my professional pursuits that the *life* of my client depended on the verdict to be taken.

"In aid of this prosecution, the honest prejudices and prepossessions of the whole community in which the crime charged against the prisoners at the bar was perpetrated have been strongly enlisted, and each individual in order has been called upon the stand with his recollection scourged and his memory quickened by the ingenuity of counsel until he has been enabled to detail in the minutest manner, every suspicious act, and thoughtless expression that have escaped these unfortunate men during the whole course of their eventful lives. And in each word, thought, and deed these witnesses are made, clearly to discover, an index as legible as the handwriting upon the wall, pointing to the prisoners as the murderers of John Love.

"That so bloody a deed as the one portrayed by the learned counsel for the prosecution at the commencement of this trial and which it will not be denied, his proof has fully established, should create sympathy, and produce excitement is creditable to the moral character and humane feelings of the citizens of Boston. God forbid that my lot should ever be cast upon a community so dead to the feelings of humanity or so accustomed to the scenes of human butchery as could remain passive and unmoved amid such slaughter as has been disclosed in the evidence. No, gentlemen, the possession of our property, the preservation of our character, the enjoyment of our liberty, and even life itself must always depend, to a greater or less degree, upon the notions and opinions which the community in which we are located entertain of personal rights and in proportion to the correctness of their estimate will the honest indignation of that community pursue the hardened villain who attempts their violation.

"That John Love was most brutally mangled, butchered, and murdered at or about Boston, in this county, sometime during the course of the last winter, through human agency, we shall not attempt a denial. The proof already adduced folly establishes that fact as also that the body found on the twenty-third of February last was the body of the deceased.

"But, gentlemen, while we freely indulge the most laudable feelings of our nature, which the mangled and lacerated body of the unfortunate Love is well calculated to inspire, let me caution you against substituting that sympathy, in the place of proof, for the purpose of fixing that murder upon the prisoners at the bar.

"Does their case find no sympathy in your benevolent bosoms? Was a more solemn and interesting occurrence ever before presented to the consideration of a jury? A father and three sons, including a whole family, put on trial for the most aggravated of all offenses. And if convicted, the consequence of that conviction is to obliterate the recollection of their existence, leaving not even a name behind. But with this, you have no more to do as jurors than with the cut and mangled remains of John Love. The question submitted to your consideration and which you are called upon to determine is, whether the prisoners at the bar were, or were not, the perpetrators of that horrid deed.

"This fact you are to decide and determine upon the legal evidence to be produced on this trial and not upon the conjectures and suspicions of witnesses that have been called before you to testify nor upon any opinions you may have formed by hearing the fatal story a thousand times repeated before you took your oaths and your seats as jurors in this cause.

"A correct definition of the crime, charged in this indictment, has been given by the prosecutor in his opening remarks, and the different species of homicide has been by him correctly stated and defined—and as was premised by him, no question will arise in the progress of this trial whether the *killing* charged is *murder* or *man-*

slaughter. It is conceded by the prisoners' counsel that if the killing, in this case, is fixed by the proof upon the prisoners at the bar, it is *murder*. I shall therefore pass to the nature of the testimony upon which this prosecution is attempted to be sustained and read to you from the books something on the subject of circumstantial testimony and the rules by which it is to be applied."

Then Mr. Love proceeded to read copious extracts from law books no one has ever heard of and probably came from the old country on the nature and application of circumstantial evidence.

Once he was done educating the jurors on the finer points of the law, he continued, "If, gentlemen, it is better that ten guilty men should escape than that one innocent man should suffer, agreeable to the long-established and well-settled maxim in the history of criminal jurisprudence, it will not be denied that in a case where three or four persons are suspected of an offense, in which all are not necessarily inculpated, and from the nature of the testimony, a difficulty should arise in fixing with legal certainty, the offense upon the actual offender, it is better that all be acquitted than that the innocent should suffer with the guilty. This just, humane, and benevolent doctrine is sufficiently illustrated in the cases that have been read to you.

"Again, gentlemen—I shall assume another position in sustaining this defense, and if I succeed in satisfying you of its correctness, I trust you will hear and apply the evidence in this cause, agreeably to the doctrine it inculcates.

"The position is this. It is better that a guilty man escape the punishment due to his crimes than he should be convicted of an offense upon incompetent proof. The end does not always justify the means. In a system of laws for the regulation of society, where every offense is clearly delineated and its punishment is distinctly known, the rules of evidence and mode of proof in determining the guilt or innocence of the accused form the most important part of those laws and is to be strictly regarded by all courts and juries as the law that defines the offense and prescribes the punishment.

"And it is more dangerous to the rights of individuals to vary the well-known and long-established rules of evidence with a view to meet a particular case than it would be to suspend the operation of a statute, to favor or oppress a particular citizen. And as it regards the security of society, it matters not whether the suspension or variation of the known rule is to convict the midnight assassin or oppress the unoffending child of misfortune, wretchedness, and want. For let it be remembered that if courts and jurors should quietly suffer the salutary rules of evidence to be violated in their mistaken zeal to punish a supposed offender, the only legal refuge of conscious and unsuspecting innocence is invaded, and the lives and liberties of our citizens become subject to the whim and caprice of a corrupt and profligate judge."

Judge Walworth spoke up just then and warned the attorney against using offensive language regarding the judiciary.

"No offense inferred to the present company," Love said.

"Very well, please continue."

"Uh, this doctrine, gentlemen, if correct, I desire you should bear in mind while the testimony is unfolding before you as well as in your final deliberations upon the fate of the prisoners.

"I shall now close these remarks, gentlemen, by charging you upon the solemnity of the oath you have taken so to divest yourselves of prejudices and conjectures which the oft-repeated story of murder and barbarity necessarily engenders as that when you shall meet the prisoners at the bar, on the confines of eternity and in the assembly of a congregated world, where neither mystery, suspicion, or doubt can exist in relation to the transactions of mortals that there in the awful presence of *your* God and of *their* God, yours will be the felicity of knowing that you heard the testimony in this case with an impartial ear and found your verdict upon the evidence given on the trial."

Mr. Love then gave a short nod of his head and sat down in his heavy oaken chair, satisfied that he had explained the warning to the jurors that they should make their decision on the prisoners' guilt solely on the evidence and not by conjecture.

The first to testify on behalf of the prisoners was Dr. James Strowbridge, a physician not previously known to me. He testified that at the time of decomposition of human bodies, or any animal for that matter, there was no rule by which to determine from the state of decay or putrefaction, how long the body had been deprived of life.

He opined that a man in good health, dying without loss of blood would decay sooner than a person who was weak and emaciated. My companion, Dr. Gould, and I looked at each other, frowning in disbelief. He then continued to say that some degree of heat and moisture was requisite to facilitate the operation of decomposition, that the time it would take must always depend on circumstances, the state of health of the individual at the time of death, habits of the person, time and place of burial, and the state of the atmosphere if the grave was so shallow as to allow that to affect the body.

I agreed with some of the things he said but certainly not the estimate of time since the person had died. I wondered if he had seen the body at all to come to his conclusions. He continued saying that in the case of Love, it would appear that some of the principal arteries were separated, and consequently, almost all his blood must have been lost. (I stand corrected!) He said the body had been so slightly buried that probably the frost had penetrated his body, and this along with the assumed blood loss must have delayed the decay and decomposition. I shook my head with the knowledge that the defense counsel was relying on generalities rather than straight facts, which I had testified to the day before.

The defense plan on behalf of the prisoners was short and only brought ten witnesses to bear. Each witness took perhaps five minutes to say what he or she knew, and most of the time, the defense counsel tried to disprove their recollections as being not correct. Many times, the district attorney objected to the testimony as being frivolous or presumptuous. Most of the time, the judge agreed. As it was, the testimony of all was considered of no consequence by the prosecutor and the judge. I actually felt that the prisoners' attorneys did a very poor job of proving that their clients did not commit this heinous crime.

Ebenezer Griffin, Esq., in his closing comments, addressed the jury on behalf of the prisoners and carried on for one hour and a half. Then a second defense attorney, Ethan B. Allen, Esq., closed the defense of the two brothers in a speech that took nearly the same amount of time. By the time they were done, most people in the room had either left or were not able to stop their nodding heads from showing their boredom.

Chapter 4, Part 3

THE ARGUMENT OF
SHELDON SMITH, ESQ

The attorney for the people, Sheldon Smith, Esq., then got up and addressed the jury, solidifying the prosecutor's case.

"May it please the court, gentlemen of the jury. I rise to address you on this occasion, under a peculiar sense of inability to do justice to a cause of such magnitude. After an incessant and laborious investigation of the last two days, I find myself too far exhausted to enter upon the discussion of a cause embracing such a vast variety of circumstances and involving interests so deep and so vital. I feel conscious that in attempting to perform the part, which falls to my lot in this matter, I must fall far short of what the public has—a right to expect—and what my duty requires. But relying on your candor and your indulgence, I shall proceed to reply to the able and eloquent arguments which have been offered on the part of the prisoners and to which I must acknowledge I have listened with equal pleasure and respect. And while I attempt to lay before you the nature and merits of this prosecution on the part of the people and to illustrate those principles of law and rules of evidence, which I consider as applicable to this case and which are usually made to govern such a state of facts as is before you, may I be permitted to hope that I shall be able in some measure to facilitate your inquiries, that my efforts, feeble as they may be, will afford you some little aid in performing the arduous, painful, and solemn duty that devolves upon you.

"The station which you occupy today is the most exalted and awfully responsible of any, and it is to be hoped in which you ever have been or can be placed. The duty you have to perform is thrown upon you by your relative situation as members of society. And although it may be laborious and painful, the consolation you will derive from a faithful discharge of that duty, will I trust, yield you an ample reward. Such as hitherto been the state of society, in this highly favored country, that our courts have rarely had to sit in judgment upon crimes of so foul a nature as the one detailed before you. And it is to be hoped that the day is distant when another trial like this shall occur again to disturb the public peace, to agitate and shock the public feeling. But it is to be feared that the age in which we live is becoming more and more corrupt, that the perpetration of crimes is becoming more and more frequent.

"If this be so, it adds much to the responsibility of those who are entrusted with the administration of public justice and the preservation of public peace. Everything that we possess or consider as worth possessing in this life depends essentially upon the purity, vigilance, and firmness of our courts and our juries. They are the guardians of society. It is to them that we look for protection against all those overwhelming evils that flow from human depravity, and without their protection, our very lives are insecure. You cannot, therefore, fail of being deeply penetrated with a sense of the importance of the trust confided to you, and I will not doubt but that trust will be, by you, faithfully and conscientiously executed. If unfortunately, you had imbibed prepossessions respecting this trial, it will be your duty to discard them, so far at least as the frailty of human nature will admit.

"The remarks of the counsel for the prisoners on this point are highly worthy of your consideration. And do not, I entreat you, gentlemen, consider this caution as a censure upon you for prejudice is incident to all human nature. No man can boast an exemption from it. And the experience I have had in courts of justice has taught me that prejudice, particularly in the minds of a jury, is a most formidable foe to the administration of public justice. It exerts an insidious and powerful influence, and the mind the most under this bias is often the least conscious of its power. We wish you to try this cause, gentlemen, upon the naked facts that have been laid before you since you entered that box. And if these facts alone and independent of all other considerations are not sufficient to convince you, beyond a rational doubt of the prisoners' guilt, we entreat you to acquit them. But if these facts and circumstances are sufficient to satisfy you, beyond a reasonable doubt, that they did commit the crime with which they are charged, it will be your imperious duty to pronounce them guilty.

"The grand question for your consideration will be—Were the prisoners, in any manner, engaged or concerned in the murder of John Love? For it is perfectly immaterial who gave the fatal blow, whether they or any other person, known or unknown, provided they were actually present, aiding and assisting when the blow was given. For in that case, the law makes the blow of one the blow of all, and all who are present, aiding and assisting when a murder is committed, are equally guilty.

"The fact that there has been a murder committed, and which is necessarily made the foundation of all prosecutions of this sort, is established by the most unequivocal testimony and is, in fact, conceded by the counsel for the prisoners. It will therefore be unnecessary for me to read you the law defining the crime or showing the distinctions between murder and the other kinds of homicide.

"The murder of John Love being established to fix the crime upon the prisoners here attending, we have recourse to a train of circumstances disclosed in the testimony. But here we are met by the counsel for the prisoners with an objection to this sort of testimony.

"The learned counsel has strenuously contended against relying on presumptive evidence in capital cases and to show you the danger of resting a conviction on circumstantial testimony. For this testimony is not the law of the land. It has never been adopted by this or any other country.

"Let us, for a moment, attend to the inducements which the prisoners had to the perpetuation of this crime. Men do not act without a motive, says one of the learned counsel for the accused. Let us see if they had a motive in this case. It appears that Isaac Thayer, one of the prisoners, had confessed judgments to John Love, the deceased, in the amount of $275. This debt had been contracted by the three brothers, whose property had been shifted into Isaac's hands for the very purpose of securing that debt. Executions had been taken out, and the property of the three brothers was liable to be sold whenever Love should direct, and as they had no means of paying for that debt, they had no way to save their property from being sacrificed for payment to John Love. It is known, too, that Love had about him considerable money and other property.

"In approaching the evidence in this case, the first prominent fact that strikes our attention is the circumstance of Love being seen in the company of the accused on the evening of the fifteenth of December, which was the last time he was seen still living. He started with the accused from the house of Nelson Thayer to go to the house of Israel Thayer Jr. for the avowed purpose of staying all night. This fact is established by the testimony of four witnesses.

"Isaac Thayer, in his examination before the magistrate at the time he was arrested, admits that Love was at the house of Israel on that night, and this is the last that is ever heard of Love until his mangled body is taken from a shallow grave not thirty rods from that fatal spot. This single fact, unexplained as it is, raises a violent presumption of guilt against the accused.

"The next remarkable circumstance is the report of a gun heard on the same evening as the fifteenth of December at or near the house of Israel Thayer. This fact is proved by a great number of witnesses. And although they do not agree as to the time of the night it was heard, there can be no doubt of the fact. It would appear that this murder was the result of arrangement and premeditation. Sylvester Irish says that about the fifteenth of December, although he does not remember the exact day, Isaac brought a rifle to the witness's house under the pretense of having the barrel recut. When he was told that it could not be recut, he still left it standing behind the witness's door.

"This house is only forty rods from Israel Thayer's house. On the afternoon of the fifteenth of December, the day preceding the murder, the boy living at Israel's house is sent home to his father's to stay all night. Then in the evening, Israel's wife is sent over to Irish's for an evening's visit. On her arrival at Irish's, she finds Isaac there. Her husband immediately goes back, and soon after, Isaac goes out and does not return for some time. These seem to have been the arrangements, and this particular time was chosen because Israel had been killing hogs that day and blood would necessarily be scattered about the house.

"These facts appear to be too plain to be misunderstood. The bringing of Israel's wife to Irish's house seems to have been the signal for Isaac, who was there waiting, to seize the placed rifle previously concealed at the same house and repair to the house of Israel and commence the horrid work. Which he undoubtedly did by shooting in at the window while the other two brothers were in the house with Love, ready to give the finishing blow.

"This conclusion is rendered the more probable from the appearance of the body of the deceased when found. The body was found with a ball through the head. The skull fractured on the back part, one side of the face cleft off, apparently with an axe, and a deadly wound across the throat, severing the breath pipe from which it is evident that two or three persons must have taken each a part in the horrid act."

At this, there arose a round of gasps and murmurs at the laying out of a very graphic picture of what must have happened. This explanation of how each brother took turns hacking and murdering the unsuspecting Love that night positively made my skin crawl and made my stomach try to regurgitate my last meal.

"Here, gentlemen, I might rest this case, satisfied that these facts would be sufficient to warrant you in pronouncing the prisoners guilty. But there are other circumstances that must not be omitted. One of the most remarkable of which is the transfer of Love's property from his possession to that of the Thayers. No sooner is Love missing than the prisoners become suddenly and unaccountably in possession of Love's property, even the very horse on which he rode to the place of his death. His horse is found in the stable of Israel Thayer, who claims it as his own.

"Nor is the means by which they got possession of some of his property unworthy of your consideration. They forged orders and a general power of attorney, authorizing Isaac Thayer to collect John Love's debts. This power of attorney they produced in courts of justice and proved genuine by their own oaths when necessary. One of these forged orders allegedly from John Love bears the date of the sixteenth of December, the very day he was murdered. So the body of the deceased was hardly cold beneath the turf before they were ransacking the neighborhood in search of his property and eagerly grasping their blood-stained fingers on all they could find."

Mr. Smith's oratory of the facts of the story showed an evil intent and carrying out of the foulest of deeds perpetuated by these brothers who the people knew for years and never could guess what they were capable of. My heart was crying for their unsuspecting wives and later on their children when faced with a future unbefitting of good Christian people.

Smith continued, "From a state of poverty and distress, harassed by constables and unable to satisfy their basest of wretched desires, they became suddenly clear of debt and flush with money. These, gentlemen, are the facts on which we rely to establish the prisoners' guilt. With such a train of guilt-proclaiming facts before us, all tending to the same point, all conspiring to establish the same awful truth, who will take it upon him to decry the power of circumstantial testimony or say that it is not equal to positive proof?"

The men in the jury box shifted their feet and recentered themselves in their seats with a look not unlike that of a child being counseled against lying or other fabrications against the truth. This is what it was coming down to—the terrifying realization that three brothers within their community had purposefully and methodically conspired to end someone's life, a life well-known by many in the community, well-known to be a generous and affable man, to end his very existence and steal everything he owned.

Again, Smith wasn't done, "The murder of John Love was one of peculiar atrocity. The most corrupt ages of the world hardly furnish its parallel. It was committed under the most aggravated circumstances and without excuse or palliation. Love was the friend of his murderers. He had lent them money and shown them many favors. On that fatal night which proved his last, they decoyed him to one of their houses as a friend and a guest, and there butcher him in cold blood as they had done their hogs the day before. They then rifle his pockets and proceed to purloin all his effects to be found in the neighborhood, adding robbery and theft to the crime of murder. Nor does their career of iniquity end there.

"Ascertaining that he had money in the hands of other persons, they proceed to collect those monies by means of forged papers and protect themselves by swearing in the name and presence of God, whose laws they thus had violated, that those papers were genuine. What a dismal catalog of crimes do we here behold! Murder, robbery, theft, forgery, and finally perjury all committed in the course of a few days by the same persons and to attain the same object, namely the acquisition of a few hundred dollars in money and property. If there be any part of this transaction more strange and unnatural than the rest, it is the hardness of heart, the blindness of mind, and the perverseness of soul, which characterized these men in their mad, unhallowed career.

"It is rare that the perpetrators of high crimes appear so perfectly steeled against all the compunctions of conscience. The murderer is usually so sure of himself until he has actually done the fatal deed. But when he has given the deadly blow and sees the victim of his malice fall and gasp beneath his feet, his courage fails him and he relents. He begins to reflect on the enormity of his crime and guilt and remorse with all their soul-tormenting horror, seize upon him, thrill through every nerve, and pierce his heart with insupportable anguish. He flees from society and shuns the face of man. He hears, or thinks he hears, from frowning heaven, the awful reproof, 'What is this that thou hast done? The voice of thy brother's blood cries to me from the ground!' But the murderers of Love seem to have been beyond the reach of those feelings. They rushed heedlessly on, from crime to crime, until they had reached a most awful and appalling climax of guilt.

"Gentlemen, as I am to be followed by other counsel, I am not disposed to detain you longer. I have endeavored to discharge my duty in this matter, in such a manner as to satisfy my conscience. And if I have evinced more zeal than may be thought compatible with the accusing side of this prosecution, I earnestly ask, that it may be ascribed to a habit of speaking and a sense of duty, rather than any improper motive or want of feeling toward the accused.

"For had I been at liberty to indulge my sympathies toward the accused, I could have wept over their misfortune and fate. But I was not at liberty to do so. The public good is, and ought to be, an object paramount to every other consideration.

"When we see the very neighborhood in which we live, infested with crimes at which humanity recoils, we ought to feel alarmed. And every citizen who participates in the benefits of the social compact ought to feel willing to see the offenders brought to justice and to perform such part as the laws of this country may assign him with firmness and fidelity. Should such offenses escape detection and punishment, the most alarming consequences might well be apprehended.

"Encouraged by the imbecility and imperfection of human laws, the felon would crawl from his hiding place and extend his depredations far and wide. A few dollars about the person of the citizen would only expose him to the rude and blood-stained hands of the assassin and the cutthroat. Society would lose all its endearments and become prey to fear, alarm, distrust, and crime."

Looking at Isaac and Israel, sitting next to their impotent attorneys, they shrunk themselves down to a mere ball of flesh and looked haggard and worn as an old shoe and probably wished that Mr. Smith would cease the onslaught of words, which he was aiming at them. They were the sorriest two men I had ever seen.

Mr. Henry Brown, Esq. then addressed the jury on the part of the people in an able speech of nearly an hour in length. The jury was released about eleven o'clock in the evening, under an elaborate and solemn charge from his honor, Judge Walworth, and in about half an hour returned to tell the judge their verdict—guilty as charged.

The verdict and sentencing of the three accused men would not be announced until the following Monday. My companion and I discussed whether to stay in Buffalo until then or head back home. We decided that we had already invested a great deal of our time in witnessing the tragedy of this trial and go back home now, only to return Sunday night, and finding lodging for one more night would be too much of a strain on our horses. So we engaged the rooming house for another three nights so we could be witnesses to the judge's admonitions and sentencing of the three men who had been found guilty of this heinous crime against a citizen of God's creation.

Chapter 5

The Verdict and Sentence

On Monday, the twenty-fifth of April 1825 at 10:00 a.m., the prisoners were brought to the courtroom to receive the sentence of the law.

Judge Walworth spoke to them in a firm and calm way, "Nelson Thayer, Israel Thayer Jr., and Isaac Thayer—you have been indicted by the grand jury of this county for the murder of John Love in the Town of Boston on the fifteenth of December last. You have respectively had fair and impartial trials in which you have been aided by faithful and intelligent counsel. After a deliberate and patient investigation of your several cases, by petit juries, they have been constrained and compelled by their consciences and their oaths to pronounce each and all of you guilty of a most foul and aggravated murder. Have you or either of you anything to say why the sentence of the law should not be pronounced against you in pursuance of your conviction for this offense?"

All three of the accused men looked down helplessly until Isaac spoke up, "Your Honor, we all have wives and children. Who shall care for them after we are gone?"

The judge sat back in his chair and looked very sad as he said, "You should have thought of that before you committed these heinous crimes."

Both men again forced their weeping eyes to the floor.

The judge continued, "The feelings and emotions with which I enter upon the discharge of the solemn and important duty which devolves upon the court and which I am now about to perform are too painful to be expressed. To pronounce the dreadful sentence which is to cut a fellow mortal off from society, to deprive him of existence, and to send him to the bar of his Creator and his God, where his everlasting destiny must be fixed for eternity, is at all times and under any circumstances most painful to the court. But to be compelled, at one and the same time, to consign to the gallows three young men who have just arrived at manhood, standing in the relation to each other as brothers and connected with society in the tender relations of children, brothers, husbands, and fathers presses upon my feelings with a weight which I can neither resist nor express.

"If in the discharge of this most painful duty that can ever devolve on any court, I should in portraying the horrid circumstances of this case make use of strong language to express the enormity of your guilt and the deep depravity which it indicates, I wish you to rest assured it is not with any intention of wounding the feelings of your relatives or for the purpose of adding one pang to your own afflictions while the righteous hand of an offended God is pressing so heavily upon you. But it will be for the purpose, if possible, to awaken you to a proper sense of your awful situation and to prepare you to meet the certain and ignominious death which shortly awaits you. It is to endeavor, if possible, to soften your hearts and to produce a reformation in your feelings that by contrition and repentance, you may be enabled to shun a punishment infinitely more dreadful than any that can be inflicted by human laws—the eternal and irretrievable ruin of your guilty souls."

The few people who stayed the weekend to hear the verdict were riveted in their seats to hear what more the judge would say. Everyone was exhausted—the judge, the jury, the prisoners, and those in the gallery. The judge made it sound like the brothers' future was a foregone conclusion. But we all wanted to hear how the judge would send this message to them after so much testimony from so many.

The judge continued, "From the testimony which was given on the trials of your several cases, there is no room to doubt the certainty of your guilt or the aggravated circumstances attending the perpetration of the bloody deed. The man whom you have murdered was your companion and friend. He had loaned you money to relieve your necessities and to support your families. He was the lenient creditor, renewing and exchanging his judgments and his executions from time to time to prevent the sacrifice of your property. He was the lodger of your father and frequently enjoyed the hospitalities of your own roofs. In the unsuspecting hour of private confidence, you decoyed him to the retired dwelling of Israel Thayer Jr., and there while he was enjoying the hospitality of the social fireside, you stole upon him unperceived—you aimed the deadly rifle at his head and with the fatal axe you mangled and murdered your victim, mingling his blood with that of your butchered swine.

"But your guilt and depravity did not stop there. Scarcely had you committed his lifeless corpse to its shallow grave before you began to collect and riot upon the spoils of his property. To the crime of murder, you added those of theft, fraud, and forgery and repeatedly imprecated the vengeance of heaven upon your perjured souls.

"The punishment of death has been denounced against the crime of murder, not only by the laws of all civilized nations but also by that law which was written by the pen of inspiration under the dictation of the unerring wisdom of the Most High. And as God himself has prescribed the righteous penalty for this offense, so there is strong reason to believe that very few murders are committed, which are not ultimately discovered, and the wicked perpetrators thereof brought to merited punishment.

"High crimes are generally perpetrated with secrecy and caution, usually in the dead of night, as in this case, when the world is wrapped in silence and sleep, when darkness covers the wretch and his deeds from every mortal eye. To require the testimony of eyewitnesses to convict in such cases would be to give all felons full license to extend their ravages at will, to prowl upon the community unde-tected and unrestrained.

"Wretched and deluded men! In vain was the foul deed perpe-trated under cover of darkness of the night, in vain was the mangled body of your murdered companion committed to the earth and the lonely grave concealed by rubbish, in vain was the little boy sent home to his mother and the unsuspecting wife removed from her house that no human eye should be near to witness the foul and unnatural murder, and in vain did you expect the snows of winter to conceal the grave until the body of your victim could no longer be known and recognized."

"You forgot that the eye of your God was fixed upon you. The eye of that God who suffers not even a sparrow to fall without his notice. You forgot that you were in the presence of him to whom the light of day and the darkness of midnight are the same, that he witnessed your movements, that he could withhold the accustomed snows from falling on the earth, or his breath could melt them when fallen, leaving the grave uncovered and thus exposing you to detec-tion and condemnation. His vengeance has, at length, overtaken you. The sword of human justice trembles over you and is about to fall upon your guilty heads, you are about to take your final leave of this world and to enter upon the untried retributions of a never-end-ing eternity."

I sat entranced by the judge's words; I trembled as if it was me he was talking to. I looked over at the prisoners and was astonished at the nonchalance and disinterest they were showing in response to being told that the Lord saw what they did and would smite them for their misdeeds. They had no fear whatsoever of what the judge was saying. I sat back in my seat, unable to fathom how anyone could be so barren.

"I beg of you not to delude yourselves with vain hopes of par-don, which never can be realized. Your destiny for this world is fixed, and your fate is inevitable. Let me, therefore, entreat you individu-ally and collectively by every motive, temporal and eternal, to reflect upon your present situation and the certain death that shortly awaits you. There is but one who can pardon your offenses, there is a Savior whose blood is sufficient to wash from your soul the guilty stains, even of a thousand murders. Let me, therefore, entreat you to fly to him for that mercy and that pardon which you must not expect from mortals."

"When you shall have returned to the solitude of your prison, where you will be permitted to remain for a few short weeks, let me entreat you by all that is still dear to you in time—by all that is dreadful in the retribution of eternity, that you seriously reflect upon your personal situation and upon the conduct of your past lives. Bring to your minds all the aggravated horrors of that dreadful night when the soul of the murdered Love was sent unprepared into the presence of its God, where you must shortly meet it as an accusing spirit against you."

"Bring to your recollections the mortal struggles and dying groans of your murdered friend. Recollect the horror which seized you while you dragged the mangled remains to the place of concealment. Think of the situation of your aged father to whom you are indebted for your existence. Think of the grief of your distracted and disconsolate mother, who has nursed you in the lap of affection and watched over the tender years of your infancy, who must now go down to the grave sorrowing over the ruins of her family."

"Think of the dreadful agonies, think of the unnatural and desolate widowhood to which you have reduced the unfortunate partners of your beds and your bosoms. Think upon the situation of your poor orphan children, on whom you have entailed everlasting disgrace and infamy and who are now to be left fatherless and unprotected to the mercy of the world."

At this final admonition, the prisoners' eyes began overflowing with tears, and their bodies shook with grief. They looked over at their wives, who sat at the back of the room, and cried aloud, "Forgive me!"

I breathed a sigh of relief, not at the fact that these men would receive the punishment they deserved but at the fact that they were, after all, human.

The judge softened his voice and continued, "And when by such reflections as these your hard and obdurate hearts shall become softened, let me again entreat you before your blood-stained hands are raised before the judgment seat of Christ, that you fly for mercy to the arms of a Savior and endeavor to seize upon the salvation of his cross.

"Listen now to the dreadful sentence of the law and then farewell forever until the court and you, with all this assembled audience, shall meet together in the general resurrection.

"You and each of you are to be taken from hence to the prison from whence you came, and from thence to the place of execution, and there, on the seventeenth day of June next, between the hours of twelve at noon and two o'clock in the afternoon, you are to be hanged by the neck until you are dead."

And in an even stronger voice said, "And may that God, whose laws you have broken and before whose dread tribunal you must then appear, have mercy on your souls."

The room was as quiet as a sleeping mouse. I fear all who were there felt the slap that was intended for the prisoners; the finality of the sentence sucked all the air out of the room and left everyone dazed. After the shock had left their bodies, the three brothers started once again to weep; their cries swelling together into a wail that reached the rafters of the courthouse and threatened to tear the very roof off. It was a very long moment before I could breathe again.

The constables took the trio of brothers by the arms and led them back to the jail where they would spend more than the next few hours contemplating what they had done, not only to themselves but to everyone they knew.

It was over. The trial was over, and three brothers had been sentenced to hang for murder. And for me, it was the end to the idea that there was good in every human soul—for there wasn't.

Chapter 6

Dr. Ingalls and Dr. Gould Return to Boston After the Trial

When discussing our return plans after the trial, Emmons mentioned that he would be interested in traveling back home through East Evans to visit a friend of ours, Dr. George Sweetland. He had just started his practice there three years ago, and we knew that his wife had recently had a child.

"What a grand idea!" I said.

I hadn't seen George in two years since he opened his practice. Evans was a farming community just like Boston, and they had been searching for a doctor to set up practice in their little village. I helped him stock his office with the bare essentials that would be needed to take care of simple illnesses and injuries. George and I had graduated a year apart from the University of Buffalo Medical School. I couldn't wait to discuss the exciting new things that would be available to doctors once the Erie Canal opens up. Also, the long ride back home would be more pleasant if we had an agreeable side trip to break up the monotony of the ride home.

The day seemed warmer than most in the month of April when we started out. We took the road out of Buffalo southward that followed the lakeshore. Off we went, the ugliness of the trial behind us, and the punishment meted out to the boys in a few months' time. It was a sad day past, but it would be the saddest of days for the family of the accused.

We started out around 7:00 a.m. as the trip to Evans would take around seven hours to travel the twenty-some miles. The day was cloudy, and though the temperature as we started was warmer, the closer we got to the lakeshore, the colder it got. Huge chunks of ice could be seen battling for positions that were almost the size of wagons. As April wore on, the chunks would eventually melt away, making fishing a more pleasurable endeavor. I had not grown up here, and the expanse of the lake amazed me in that you could not even see the opposite shore; it was so far away! They said Canada was across the lake on the opposite side, and I planned one day to visit there if the opportunity to make the trip were to arise. I'm sure that lake traffic will increase substantially once the canal opens up. The opportunity to trade and sell goods from as far west as Lake Superior to as far east as New York City was simply implausible and unbelievable to me, and I would be lucky enough to see it happen in my lifetime!

"Well, sir," said Emmons, "the day began as warm and inviting, but I fear that the winds blowing over the ice have caused the temperature to dip substantially."

"I heartily agree!" I said, shivering, and turned around to the wagon behind us and grabbed the blankets we brought with us should we need them.

We wrapped them around our shoulders to block the cold and carried on.

The trail was still frozen from the long winter, so we didn't have to contend with mud bogging down our wheels as in the summer, but there were deep frozen crevasses where previous wagons had plodded during the fall rains, making long lines of little hills and valleys that our wheels kept falling into and out of. It made for a very bumpy ride for many miles.

We traveled through a few small villages along the way, some looking quite deserted as the residents were probably inside trying to stay warm. North Evans was due south of the village of Lakeview along North Creek. We talked intermittently and sang sometimes when the spirit led us, but most of the journey was spent in silence, each of us in our own thoughts, whether that be the travesty of what happened in the village of Boston, the anticipated new access to modern methods of doctoring, thinking of our loved ones on the other side of the hill, or just trying to think blank thoughts in order to erase the images of John Love's body, riddled with gunshot holes and ax gashes.

As we passed into the area now known as the Seneca Creek Reservation, the forest to the left of us was dark and gloomy. We weren't sure where the natives had put up their settlements for the winter, but they were probably inside that forest, where they could send out parties to hunt and fish. I wouldn't want to live so close to the lake in the winter; the winds can be severe, and the temperature can go down below freezing. But I suppose they are used to those conditions since they've been here a lot longer than the colonists have.

I secretly hoped we wouldn't meet up with any of them along the trail; I have heard stories of their hatred and mistrust of the colonists, and sometimes those meetings don't end well. I've tried to educate myself on their way of life, and I've wished that all people could get along together. But the reality of it is we took their land and took away their ability to farm the best land, and they have been forced to live a different way than their ancestors did to suit what we claim is the "civilized" way to live. We tried to get them to change their religion—to be "Christians" in the way we are used to believing in God; instead of their belief in their "Great Spirit" and the idea that their god is evidenced in everything from rocks to birds to fish. They call the land their "Mother," and that life is all about living in harmony with nature as a whole. When you really think about it, who are we to say that's wrong? Thousands of their people had been forced to leave the land that was their father's and their father's fathers throughout time. I suppose I would not be happy with the people who might do that to me and my people. Even so, if we saw any Iroquois, we would give them a wide berth and behave respectably.

Some of the spring birds were arriving from their winter homes, and we could hear them twittering and calling from the forest. It had been a long and trying winter—I was looking forward to the freshness of spring and the anticipation of new growth, both in the flowers and crops and the birth of baby animals and humans alike and in opportunities that the canal would bring our community.

Living in the wilderness of Northwestern New York State was difficult. As a physician, not having access to the new treatments for even the most basic of ailments meant that more children would die of lung disease and women from consumption. I can't treat an infection with the most modern pharmaceuticals. I have read about some new treatments in books, but it was always a diaphanous dream to actually have the chance to purchase some of these new medicines and bring my profession into the nineteenth century! Now with the canal's opening just months away, I can save more lives and make people more comfortable as they heal from whatever malady that befalls them.

There are no dwellings of any kind along the trail to East Evans, just miles and miles of forest and thicket. As we move away from the lake, the temperature gets warmer, and we can put the blankets back in the wagon. I'm very glad we brought them.

Late afternoon approached and we saw a building in the distance. As we got closer, we saw it was a little village, and the building we saw was a small tavern. We looked at each other and smiled—we wouldn't have to eat the hardtack we brought with us—we could get a warm meal at the tavern. We brought the horses to a stop and gave them water. They could rest while we went inside.

We entered the tavern and were met with warm greetings and salutations. There were three or four other travelers there as well as two men who ran the place; three or four tables and sets of chairs scattered about the dark room with lanterns on each table. We requested a drink and some meat and bread as we took a couple of chairs at one of the sparse tables. We listened as the tavern owner was regaling two of the travelers with a story about how he came to move here and open a tavern. We learned later that his name was Nathaniel Hurd. He was telling the travelers a heart-wrenching story of how he had owned a tavern in the village of Buffalo and how he and his family had barely escaped their home with their lives when the British came and burned the whole village down in December of 1813. He and his wife and three children lost their home and business to the conflagration and escaped to the village of Tonawanda, where they had relatives with not much more than the clothes on their backs. A neighbor had come banging on their door and warned them that the British were marching toward the village, and they should best leave or be killed! The women and children only had time to grab some family mementos, some household goods, some rations, and blankets as Nathaniel hitched their horses to a wagon and then had his family climb on to run for their lives. That night, British Lt. General Gordon Drummond burned the whole village to the ground. His men shattered windows and threw torches into the homes and businesses. One of their neighbors, Sarah Lovejoy, they heard, had not fled the scene and tried to protect her home and belongings. Nathaniel heard that one of the Natives who came with the British had killed her with a tomahawk. His children lost their pet dog and the few toys that they had received for Christmas. It was a brutal story. They ended up staying the winter with relatives in a small cabin with an aunt, uncle, and cousins.

"Friend," I said to Nathaniel, "that is one of the most harrowing of stories I have heard in recent memory. However, did you not succumb to such a huge loss in your lives? How did you have the strength to move on and build here?"

"By the grace of God!" he exclaimed. "And by all the pints of beer I've consumed since then to forget that it ever happened!"

The room rang with laughter, although some of the sounds were of nervous laughter. Surviving such an ordeal meant that he was a strong man with strong convictions and strong beliefs. One of the travelers in the room spoke to me later and confessed that he had known Nathaniel for some years now, and he had learned a great deal from the man's strengths. I then knew that Nathaniel was perfectly suited to tame this wilderness that we lived in.

I was bolstered by the camaraderie of those in the room. The men here were proof that the oft-time tragedies that befall those who venture into the wilderness to make a new life for themselves and their families need not break a man—that with struggle comes strength and with hard work and diligence comes success. I was glad we had happened upon this tavern on our way to East Evans.

After we supped, we proceeded to ask Nathaniel if he had a room we could rent overnight. The conversation was engaging, and we did not want to interrupt the amity of the room, but we were tired and needed some rest. Besides, a nice warm bed was preferable to a cold night in the wagon. He did have a room for the two of us, and we retired to that place after bidding our hosts a safe and good night.

In the morning, we had a hearty breakfast that Nathaniel's wife had graciously cooked for us, and we bid farewell to Nathaniel and his family and prayed that we would once again enjoy his company. We left with the knowledge that we knew there were some fine men in this area that we could call friends.

The morning was a fine one and we were glad for the sun greeting us. We gathered our now-rested horses and continued on the path to East Evans, where we would visit our friend George. As we traveled away from the lake, we no longer had to contend with the cold wind. The rhythmic plodding of the horses' hooves on the still frozen ground was somehow hypnotic as the miles went by; kind of like sitting next to a grandfather clock and hearing the secondhand tick over and over. One could almost hear one's heartbeat matching the rhythm of the horses' steps, lulling one into a twilight of consciousness bordering on waking sleep. Our bellies were full of the fine breakfast we had enjoyed, and the sun was beating down on us, melting the frozen dew on the grasses assisted in a feeling of comfort.

Suddenly, upon the noon hour, both horses snorted and lost the rhythm of their step. I started into wakefulness and immediately looked around to try to determine the cause of the horse's change in rhythm. Emmons, in the meantime, also started awake and uttered a weak shout that broke the silence.

Up ahead on the path, perhaps fifty rods away, stood a lone rider. His horse was stopped and was looking at us with a calm demeanor. I could not make out the rider and the clothes he wore at first. Our horses had also stopped, so I gave the reins a slap and started them moving again. He also urged his horse forward to meet us.

As we got closer, my heart quickened when I saw the hawk feathers on the horse's bridle. I could see that the rider wore a blanket over his shoulders, and his horse was saddleless. The man's face appeared dark, and his graying hair was long and gathered at the neck on either side of his head. He carried a bow and arrows on his back and a rifle by his side. A shiver of fright ran down my spine. Was it an Iroquois? Was he really alone, or were there others hidden in the forest where we could not see? Were we going to have trouble here? I tried to collect myself before speaking.

"Hello, friend!" I said.

His horse had stopped just to the right of our team of horses but kept his distance. Up close, the man appeared to be older—perhaps sixty. His clothing and his horse were immaculate. The horse's coat had been brushed to a chestnut gleam. The man, an Indian, sat very straight on the horse's back, even in the absence of a saddle. He was wrapped in a multicolored blanket, intricate jacquard stripes in hues of cream, orange, and dark brown. As a child, I learned some of the patterns different tribes used when making their blankets, and this one appeared to be of the Seneca tribe. The Senecas were farmers, not known for warring with the colonists. His face did not exude any hostility or sternness. I decided that I did not think we had anything to fear from him.

After an awkward silence in which he seemed to conclude that we were also no threat to him, he introduced himself. "I am Sagoyewatha of the Seneca Nation. I am chief of the Wolf clan. The White man calls me Red Jacket."

"Greetings, great warrior," Emmons declared suddenly.

I gave a start at his voice which was the first time he had spoken all morning.

"I have heard great stories of your courage and travels. It is an honor to meet you here. What brings you here this far west?"

As Emmons was conversing with the man, I realized we were in the presence of a legend. I felt a little mistrust of him though, knowing that he had received his White man name because of the red British military jacket given to him by the British during the Revolutionary War. At that time, the Seneca had sided against the colonists and gave their allegiance to the British. I remember being taught as a young student how Red Jacket had then met with President George Washington, who awarded him with a large silver peace medal for his negotiations on behalf of the Seneca people after the war. Although the Seneca were forced to cede much of their land to the colonists, through his efforts, they were able to retain some measure of their territory in the land we had traveled this morning—the Buffalo Creek Reservation. My eyes fell on the silver inlaid half-stock long rifle at his side and realized it was the very same rifle presented to him by President Washington. Yes, Red Jacket was a fierce supporter of his people and therefore best respected—at a distance perhaps.

He obviously was not going to tell us his destination—his silence made that clear. Instead he merely raised his head and said, "What of you?"

"We are headed to Boston, by way of East Evans," explained Emmons, pointing to himself and me. "We were in attendance at the trial of the three Thayer brothers who had been accused of killing their boarder. They were found guilty and will be hanged in Buffalo in a few months."

"I have heard of it. They will suffer a dishonorable death. Foolish White man—killing over money. Battle is the place to see men die" was all he said.[2]

After an awkward pause on all parties' part, we went our separate ways.

Red Jacket nodded to us and said something I wasn't expecting, "I hope the Great Spirit will protect you on your journey and return you safely to your friends." Then he led his horse back slowly in the direction we had just come from.

---

[2] *History of the City of Buffalo and Erie County, with Illustrations 1620–1884*, Vol. I, edited by H. Perry Smith (D. Mason & Co., 1884).

We had just experienced a memorable meeting with the only Native American we met on the path back to Boston.

We continued on our way to East Evans and the home of George Sweetland. We arrived just after the noon hour. He was seeing a patient at the time, a young man who had cut his hand while working on his father's farm. He spied us through the door as we approached and, with great excitement at seeing us, quickly wrapped gauze around the wound and secured it with a metal clasp. George told the young man to say hello to his mother and father for him then sent him on his way.

"Why, Dr. Daniel Ingalls and Dr. Emmons Gould! What brings you to my humble home?" he exclaimed, shaking hands firmly all around. "Sit! Please sit!"

We brought three chairs together from his waiting room and settled in telling him the story of our travels so far since Buffalo.

"My! What an experience to go through! Was the courtroom full?"

"I think the whole town of Boston was there!" I exclaimed. "I was the first to testify. I had to sit up at the front of the room with the judge and the district attorney and explain how I determined the cause of death and what my findings were. Friend, I was really nervous. I had to clear my throat several times before I could get any words out. The gallery was so hushed and quiet. I think if someone had sneezed, we all would have jumped out of our seats. The tension in the room was so palpable."

"How did people react to your testimony? Did it seem that they were able to understand everything you were saying?" asked George.

"Well, the wounds were graphic to explain, to say the least. Once or twice, I heard a woman or two gasp at the gruesomeness. Do you know that after they shot him, they then swung an axe at his head and broke his neck?"

George shook his head and looked down at his feet. "How horrible!" he said. "And this was back in December, you say?"

"Yes, I received a letter from the Boston Constable in February, telling me that the townspeople had discovered the body of their friend and asked me to oversee the autopsy. I had several patients suffering from lung ailments at the time, so I asked my wife to see to their care while I was gone. She's a good girl. I couldn't ask for a better nurse.

"I hitched up Matilda to the wagon and set off the next morning. Along about forenoon, I arrived at the small North Boston schoolhouse where they had the body kept. They had a fire going in the woodstove, but they couldn't keep it too warm as the body might defrost to the point of rot—he had been dead since late December."

"Of course, of course," agreed George.

I knew I could be frank with my fellow physicians; they understood the situation thoroughly. We had all been through autopsies before—although those other times were usually a natural death, not a contrived death at the hand of someone else.

We continued sharing our experience with George when his wife came to the door with their new baby to say hello. We discontinued our graphic discussion and focused on admiring the little one who was just "cute as a button," as they say. She was sleeping in her mother's arms as comfortably as she must have felt in the womb. I admitted that I would like to hold her, but I didn't want to interrupt her sleep.

"Nonsense," George's wife, Susan, said. "She needs to wake for her next feeding anyway."

She was but a month old, bless her heart, and couldn't have been more than six or seven pounds. She stirred with the transfer from her mother to me, but she didn't fuss—yet. She opened her eyes and blinked a couple of times, then her face started to turn red, and I anticipated the sharp cry of an infant taken away from her mother's warmth. The silence was broken by her wail in which she realized that she was indeed due for some nourishment. I handed her back to her mother, laughing.

"Sometimes I have that effect on people," I said.

We all had a good chuckle.

After we had visited for several more hours and shared our current lives with each other, Susan came back and invited us to sup with the family. We did not want her to go out of her way on our account, but she insisted that it was no trouble. She had also made preparations for us to stay the night and get a fresh start for Boston in the morning.

The weather outside had become rather snowy while we talked, so again, we were happy to have a place to stay rather than drive the horses through the snow and the dark.

The dinner was quite satisfying, and we wanted nothing else. Susan was a fine wife, and we were happy for George in his new surroundings and status within the town.

The next morning, we awoke to a slight overnight dusting of new snow on the ground and the sun shining down, threatening to melt it all as if it had never been there. Susan prepared a morning meal for us and even packed us some sandwiches for the trip home. We started the final leg of our journey over and through the small village of Eden, over the south Boston hill, and back to North Boston, where we had met up together some six days previously. We bid each other good health and safe travels as each of us ventured back to our homes. We wouldn't see each other again until the day came for the hangings in Buffalo on June 17, 1825.

Chapter 7

THE HANGINGS

June seventeenth, the year of our Lord 1825. That was the day that Judge Walworth designated for the punishment to be meted out to the guilty—Nelson Thayer, Isaac Thayer, and Israel Thayer Jr. They had all been found guilty on the twenty-fifth of April last, of the crime of murder. The evidence from the trial and the testimony of the witnesses arrived at the following conclusions:

They had contemplated the act four or five weeks previous and decided that December 15th would be the day they would do it. Not only had they planned it ahead of time, but they all committed some heinous part of the deed against John Love. The boy who stayed with them, Daniel Pierce, was to be sent home, and Israel's wife was convinced to go visit the Irish's. They planned on enticing Love to come to Israel's house while they were butchering hogs. Isaac had left a rifle outside of the window and planned on shooting Love as he sat by the fire warming his feet. Nelson and Israel were cutting up the pork on the stoop and moved inside to the fire to finish the final cutting into supper-sized portions.

Then as Love was sitting at the fire with his boots off, Isaac shot him in the head from outside the house. Being as he was nervous about the whole thing, he hadn't aimed very well, and it was just a glancing blow. Nelson knew his brother might chicken out, so he and Israel were prepared to finish Love off in case his aim went astray. As soon as he was hit by the bullet, he did not fall, but he snapped to attention and sat upright in the chair. Nelson then violently inflicted a wound behind his ear with the meat ax and then struck a second blow to the back of his head, which was the final blow that threw him prostrate on the floor. Just for good measure, Nelson struck him several more times in the face, which was evidenced by the damage I attested to at the trial. As the blood from his wounds mingled on the floor with the blood of the hogs, Nelson and Israel realized he was finally dead and dragged him out to the porch of the house and on down to the end of the building. They then finished off the butchering they had planned for the day.

Isaac, after firing off the rifle, went directly to Sylvester Irish's house to collect his wife and stayed there until his brothers would meet up with him. Nelson and Israel cleaned up the blood off of the floor, but the chair he had been sitting on was stained beyond the ability to clean it, so they placed some of the bloody cut-up pork on the chair, so they could mingle the blood on it. Then later, Israel's wife would clean it thinking it had been stained from the cut meat.

After the attempt to clean the blood and cover their crime, they took up Love's body and carried it to a ravine and frozen brook in the back of the house. They tried burying him in the brook but, after a few minutes of digging, discovered it was too rocky. So they dragged the body to the side of the ravine and covered it with rocks and brush whereupon it was discovered in February.

Being a doctor, I spent my life healing people. But there was a strange intrigue being whispered around town about wanting to attend the hangings to see the brothers punished for their crimes. The three men did not have a good rapport with the community, so no one felt sorry for them. There have always been hangings before; it was the accepted method of punishment, especially for this kind of crime, and it was surprisingly popular event to witness for many people, but I generally found them very distasteful. I believed in the goodness of man, that with the right amount of attention and training, one could learn not to hate and how to find lawful solutions to conflict. Maybe that's just a hopeful design, but deep inside, I wanted to believe in it.

Many people, including my friend Emmons, had asked me the previous week if I was going to Buffalo to see the hangings. I supposed that if I witnessed the punishment the brothers were due to receive, it would be like completing an unpleasant chore that was best to just bite the bullet and get it done. I began the chore by completing the autopsy on the body then testified and relayed my findings to the court. Seeing them punished for taking Love's life would complete the circle. But I couldn't get the words of Red Jacket whom we had met a few months earlier out of my head when he said, "Battle is the place to see men die."

After many days and hours of soul-searching, I decided that I would witness this event and hope that the sight would deter anyone who would think of committing a crime, knowing what the punishment would be. We hitched up the wagon on June 16 and headed north along with a wagon train consisting of seven others from Boston to get to Buffalo later in the day. It was a seven-hour trip, and the weather couldn't have been better for sitting through the twenty-five-some-mile trek.

It was an uneventful trip if you don't count meeting several dozen other wagons making the same journey. I had never seen so many wagons lined up to get to the same destination before. Though some of the souls were raucous, most were somber and reflective. The raucous ones seemed to be drinking and carrying on about how exciting it will be to witness the only probable triple hanging in Buffalo history. I thought it reflected poorly on their character as they caroused in front of women who may have been reluctant to be there in the first place.

As we approached the village, there were more and more people on the road. It was astounding! They started slowing the progress of the line of wagons to the point that we were barely moving at all. Indeed, hundreds of people were snaked on the road to the village. Military guards were flanked on either side of the road. What began as a hesitant trip to see an unsavory event became a circus of humanity charged up and ranting as they approached the corner of Court St., just west of Niagara Square. From afar, I could see the gallows rising from the ground—a huge spectacle that must have taken days to build—in order to accommodate the three ropes and trapdoors that would send the men on the last trip they would ever experience. I shuddered as I was regretting my decision to come here.

We found a spot to park the wagon that was not far enough away from the throng for my tastes but still within sight of the gallows. Other wagons were stopped, and I could smell campfires being lit to cook a meal before they bunked in their wagons for the night. The sky was clear of clouds, and the cacophony of stars was clearly visible. I thought then that the multitude of human beings here tonight perhaps may even outnumber the faraway specks of light. The throng finally settled down about midnight, and most people slept in their wagons or on the ground.

The next morning, I awoke just at sunrise and began to prepare some eggs, bacon, and coffee for myself and my comrades. I did not know how long the exhibition would last, and we needed nourishment to carry us to the time when we would leave this place. I was hoping it would be a brief event, so we could be on the road at least by the noon hour.

After we had eaten, we sat atop the wagon and prepared for the demonstration. We saw a wagon filled with three coffins approach the gallows and park just at the bottom of it. The crowd whispered and murmured their realization that this was about to get started. It was rumored that the wives of Nelson and Israel were stationed in a window in the home of Sheriff Littlefield on the corner of Batavia and Washington streets overlooking the gallows. As we looked on, we saw the militia march toward the gaol on Washington St. They stayed there for what seemed like hours and finally came to attention as the three brothers were led out of the building. It was nearly 2:00 p.m. They were dressed in white shrouds and trousers, and as they and the militia marched toward the gallows, the town band joined in behind playing that solemn tune, "Roslin Castle." The military stopped at the gallows and formed a hollow square around the platform steps. The rifle company comprised the front line of the square, and the three men were brought forward to ascend the steps. There were chairs set up over each trapdoor where the three were seated. There was another line of chairs set up right behind them to accommodate the minister and the sheriff. There were six men who led the prisoners, one man on each side of him, up the steps. The doomed men seemed to not have the ability to walk a straight line, which I thought odd. The six then sat down behind the prisoners. Their duty after the hangings was to gather up each body after it went through the trapdoor, cut it down, and place it in the coffins waiting in the wagon below.

The murmuring stopped when the sheriff, dressed in his crisp uniform and holding his sword on his hip, read the death warrant after which the minister preached the funeral sermon. I could not hear every word, but I could see many tears shed that attested to its wretchedness. The men were then stood up, and the chairs were removed. They then kneeled as the minister prayed with them, asking God to have mercy on their souls. Except for the minister's words, the air was totally silent; not even the birds in the thick surrounding trees made a sound. The prayer was ended, their confessions read, and the prisoners stood up. They then shook hands with those on the platform and then with each other, bidding a final goodbye. There was no struggling on the part of the prisoners that I witnessed, and I heard later that they had been bled previously to being taken from the gaol. This would have been done to weaken them and perhaps to lead them to die faster after the door dropped down from under their feet and the noose tightened around their neck. The lack of blood in their bodies would have made them dizzy, so they wouldn't come to the stark realization that they were about to die. I had heard about this process, but I had never witnessed the result. The white hoods were placed over their heads and the nooses tightened around their necks. I saw several women swoon at this sight, and their men caught them before they fell. Some other people in the crowd seemed to be straining toward the stage as if in complete wonder at the spectacle. I saw a man to our right turn his wife around after she turned her back on the horrific scene and whisper to her, "You made me bring you here all the way from Batavia, and you're going to watch!"

The awful silence was broken by the sudden realization and wailing coming from Nelson, Isaac, and Israel as the reality of their situation hit them. The sheriff stood above the rope that was holding the trapdoors in place. He raised his sword. As it glinted in the sunlight, he swung it down with a fierce wail, and…the rope was only cut by half. The three stopped wailing and steeled themselves against the anticipated fall through the floor, then when it didn't happen, wailed all the louder. He raised the sword a second time, brought it down again on the rope, and it still did not cut it wholly! In my mind, I berated the sheriff for not sharpening his sword before arriving this morning. While the wailing reached an ear-splitting pitch, he raised the sword a third time, threw it down, and cut the rope all the way, swinging the doors open and dropping the poor souls down the opening whereupon the rope would have broken their necks on the way down. The wailing had stopped, but now there was a massive exclamation from the hundreds, if not thousands, of spectators as they could finally exhale and breathe again after holding their breaths in anticipation.

The bodies were cut down and gently placed in the waiting coffins, their families surrounding the wagon, the wives gently weeping. I know not where the wagon took the bodies. Afterward I had heard two rumors—one that they were taken to the field wherein other criminals thusly punished lied. The other rumor was that the father of his three sons took them back to Boston to be buried on family land.

By the time we realized that the whole ordeal was over, it was half past three. We gathered up our things and had to wait until the spectators to the south of us began their own journey home. Finally, by the supper hour, we were able to get on to the main road back. We had brought some victuals with us to eat on the way home, but it would be past midnight when we entered the town border. Emmons took me to his home where I laid my weary head to rest until morning.

Prologue to
When Love Died

The story of John Love and the Thayer brothers is still taught to the fourth graders in Boston, New York, in their local history class to this day. There is a cast-iron historical marker located at the road in front of the property that used to belong to the Thayers in 1824.

There are no public graves for the three Thayer brothers. I would posit they were either buried in a Potter's field where they buried other criminals who were hung for their crime, or their bodies were released to their father who, it is rumored, buried them on Brother Nelson's property on the east hill above the Boston valley. I believe the latter is probably true.

The Buffalo History Museum contains old newspaper clippings and other documents related to the John Love story in their research library. One such document includes the order of Col. Potter to Capt. Smith regarding the execution of the three Thayers. The document requests the presence of the New York State Militia at the execution of the Thayer brothers in Niagara Square. The militia is asked to appear and parade, armed and equipped to prevent tumults, riots, and the rescue or escape of the convicts.

The story is kept alive further by the group "Explore Buffalo," which conducts walking tours of historic places in the city of Buffalo. One of the stops on one of their tours is Niagara Square, where the story of John Love and the hangings of the three brothers is shared at the very location where the gallows was built.

In my research, I discovered an eyewitness account of the hangings:

> I came from Batavia with my beau. There were six of us in the carriage, and I remember that the roads in all directions were crowded with people coming to the execution. It was a beautiful spring day and all about Niagara Square the trees were standing in almost a thick wood. They bled the prisoners in the jail before they brought them to the scaffold, and I can see them now as they reeled along, walking by the bearers. They were bled so that they would be less likely to strangle, and I suppose so they would die quicker… I remember that the sheriff swung his sword three times before he cut the rope that let the drop fall. Every time he swung the sword, the sun would flash on the blade, and the prisoners would dodge and wince… They fell about five feet and died. I have hardly ever gone to bed since that day sixty-eight years ago, but some part of the terrible scene comes before my eyes.

The town of Boston is still a small farming community where the hills hold acres of corn and other grain. The valley holds the business and commerce hub which still only has one stoplight, one bank, one grocery store, and no fast-food businesses. That may change sometime in the future, but I think the town will always retain its small-town feel.

References

1. *Joseph Bennett of Evans and the Growing of New York's Niagara Frontier* by Kevin H. Siepel, published by Spruce Tree Press, Angola, New York 2006.
2. *Bond of Union: Building the Erie Canal and the American Empire* by Gerard Koeppel, published by the Hachette Books, March 2010.
3. "The Trial of Israel Thayer, Jr., Isaac Thayer, and Nelson Thayer for the Murder of John Love," reported for the Publisher by James Sheldon, Counselor. Printer and published in Buffalo, New York, by H. A. Salisbury 1825.
4. Eyewitness account written by Nancy Pauline Graham 1897, found online on February 7, 2007, on http://freepages.geneology.rootsweb.com/~coddingtons/2820.htm.

Sherrie L. Pluta grew up in the hills of Boston, New York, and became aware of the John Love story in the fourth grade along with all the other students at Boston Valley Elementary during their class on local history. The stone grave marker of John Love was located at the very front of Maplewood Cemetery in the middle of town. Maplewood Cemetery was her family's destination every Memorial Day, where, along with her father and siblings, they planted flowers by the graves of her father's parents, who died when he was only six years old, and her father's aunt and uncle who adopted him after his parents' demise. Seeing the Love marker at such a young age made her curious about the reality of what really happened and was intent on researching it one day.

She began her writing experience with a book on the history of the town of Boston, New York, using photographs borrowed from the Boston Historical Society's Museum. She continues an active interest in the history of Western New York and especially in her hometown.

www.ingramcontent.com/pod-product-compliance
Lightning Source LLC
Chambersburg PA
CBHW061345160726
47995CB00001B/177